Long Branch in the Golden Age

Long Branch in the Golden Age

Tales of Fascinating and Famous People

Sharon Hazard

THE
History
PRESS

Published by The History Press
Charleston, SC 29403
www.historypress.net

Copyright © 2007 by Sharon Hazard
All rights reserved

Cover image: Band concerts were held at Ocean Park every afternoon in the summer.

First published 2007

Manufactured in the United States

ISBN 978.1.59629.216.1

Library of Congress Cataloging-in-Publication Data

Hazard, Sharon.
The golden age in Long Branch : tales of fascinating and famous people / Sharon
Hazard.
p. cm.
Includes bibliographical references.
ISBN 978-1-59629-216-1 (alk. paper)
1. Long Branch (N.J.)--Biography--Anecdotes. 2. Celebrities--New Jersey--Long Branch-
-Biography--Anecdotes. 3. Long Branch (N.J.)--History--Anecdotes. 4. Long Branch
(N.J.)--Social life and customs--Anecdotes. I. Title.
F144.L8H39 2007
974.9'46--dc22
2007006590

Contents

A Place Called Long Branch

Long Branch, New Jersey, is a town stretching along a sturdy bluff that rises above the Atlantic Ocean. According to the November 19, 1926 issue of the *Long Branch Daily Record*, the town got its name from its location on the longest branch of the Shrewsbury River, which forms its northwest border. In 1876 *Harper's Magazine* described it as looking "remarkably long and narrow, like a lady's foot." It is five miles long and a mere four miles wide. Because of its location along a twenty-foot-high bluff, Long Branch is often referred to as the American Brighton, after the popular resort of Brighton in England that has a similar topography. Even some of the streets and areas of the town are named after England's Brighton area. The easternmost section of Long Branch is called the West End after its English counterpart. The streets surrounding this area are named West End, Brighton, Chelsea and Bath after places in England.

However it is physically described, Long Branch is a place where the sea and the shore have met, sometimes peacefully and many times dramatically, long before any humans had the pleasure of leaving their footprints in the sand.

Besides this ceaseless coming together of sand and surf, through the years there have been many other meetings along this coastline. These were the interactions of people who were drawn to the sea for many reasons: some came for rest and relaxation, some for the health benefits of the sea air and others visited for business or just plain pleasure. Many of these people were rich and famous, powerful and politically connected. In addition to the noted visitors, many others were born, worked, lived, died and were buried in Long Branch. What they all had in common was an appreciation of this unique place with its unparalleled view of the ever-changing Atlantic Ocean, and the fond memories they had of their time spent here.

Many of the people who walked along the speckled sands of the city's shoreline are long forgotten. Some of them were famous in their time and their names are

Promenade on the Long Branch boardwalk. *Pat Curley Schneider.*

The Long Branch boardwalk, a hallmark of the Jersey Shore. *Author's collection.*

readily recognized. Others were popular in the era when they lived, but their names have been forgotten. Most people today don't know how important these celebrities were to Long Branch in its golden years. So many famous people visited during the mid-nineteenth and the early twentieth centuries that the *New York Times* ran a daily column on the front page called *In the Summertime*. It listed the comings and goings of the people visiting Long Branch, where they were staying, how many horses they brought with them, what kind of carriages they were driving and with whom they were socializing. *Harper's Weekly* and *Frank Leslie's Illustrated Newspaper* had reporters and artists camped out in Long Branch to cover the doings of each summer day.

The following chapters will share the stories of these people by bringing back to life Long Branch in its golden years. These pages will paint a picture of what the town looked like when vacationers strolled along the shore, danced in the hotel ballrooms, gambled large sums of money in the casinos, built magnificent mansions and socialized with the powerful people and political pundits of the time.

Earliest Visitors

Before there was enough activity in the town to warrant a complete front-page column in a national newspaper or an illustration in a weekly magazine, Long Branch had its share of visitors. In 1814, when the town had a total of only fourteen boardinghouses and hotels, a young girl was visiting: Victorine DuPont of Wilmington, Delaware. It seems she was seeking the health benefits and social activity of this town that meandered peacefully along the bluff. The letters she wrote home to her sister during the month of August gave a vivid description of the sights and sounds of her two-week stay in Bennet's Hotel in Long Branch. It was located on a corner, on the east side of the present-day Ocean and Bath Avenues. Her initial impression on her first day in residence at the hotel describes a barren land with no trees, just an expanse of brown earth rolling freely to the ocean. Apparently she came to Long Branch to get over some sort of melancholy or sadness. In a letter she wrote, "This landscape does not do much for lifting spirits. Is this the spot where the young, the gay, and the fashionable visit for amusement and to enjoy the country in the summer?" However, as her first week unfolded she began to appreciate her presence in a place so close to the sea. She wrote home that the sea presented a most beautiful sight:

I am very well pleased with it because it is something new. I love to cast my eyes on that vast expanse of water where many sails are to be seen, and also little boats which look like small specks upon the sea. All this is calculated to awaken great thoughts and to make one reflect, but I think also to improve melancholy. The noise of the waves which I hear constantly breaking upon the shore is soothing. I cannot think of a situation more calculated to improve melancholy than one on the sea coast, as you are constantly exposed to witness something which you cannot believe.

Victorine wrote daily and waited for the fish wagons coming from Fishtown, now known as North Long Branch, to pick up her letters and carry them on the seventy-mile trip to Philadelphia. The procedure was the same for those who wanted to post letters to New York City. The fish wagons would stop by the hotels to sell seafood to be served to the dinner guests before going on their way to the Fulton Street Fish Market in the city. They would deliver letters on route to the cities and pick up ones coming back to the shore.

As her stay progressed and her letters became more and more descriptive, Victorine talked about an amusement called bathing. She wrote, "It is the chief and grand business of every person." Bathing in the ocean was enjoyed by men and women. It was done for medicinal reasons as much as for recreation and refreshment. Of course, gentlemen and women did not bathe together. There were bathing sessions for men in the early morning and for the women in mid-morning. Women and men rented swimsuits from rickety, wooden concession huts that lined the beach. The swimsuits for women were known as swim-dresses. They consisted of green woolen gowns, stockings, shoes and caps. Practically no part of the female body was left exposed. Many times women chose to have men escort them down to the sea. If they did not have one readily available, they paid a young single man to do so. These men were known as "gigolos"—the name given today to a man who is supported by a woman.

During her second week in Long Branch, Ms. DuPont told her sister that she did not like the influx of visitors. She wrote that so many people were coming and going, it was like a whirlwind. There were many reasons for this convergence. The year was 1814, James Madison was president of the United States and the War of 1812 was still being waged. Victorine wrote home about the many frigates (warships smaller and faster than battleships) she saw sailing along and reiterated her dislike for the English enemy. She also didn't miss a chance to tell her sister about some of the visitors who came to stay in the immense wooden hotels clustered along the coast. Many of them were soldiers passing through on their way to Washington, D.C., one of whom was Edward Cole. He was First Lady Dolley Madison's cousin as well as secretary, confidant and war scout to President Madison. He was coming from the Canadian Front on his way to the capital, and Long Branch was a good place to stop for some rest and entertainment. Victorine told her sister that a ball was being planned in honor of the soldiers in residence at the local hotels. She and her traveling companion had been invited, but they were not sure if they would go. Apparently, the invitation came on the same day that the party was given. From Victorine's correspondence, it seems that besides attending dances and dinners, many of the ladies staying at the hotels passed their time playing billiards and bowling.

As she was about to leave Long Branch for her journey back to the Brandywine Valley in Delaware, the lure of the sea took hold and she began to feel sad about leaving. She described her final hours and was sad that she had not kept a daily journal. (Thankfully, her letters have survived and they provide a daily commentary.) On her last day, she rose early to see the sun rise over the ocean. She described the scene to her sister by writing,

> *Yesterday morning I arose at three o'clock a.m., being determined to see the sun rise; as we were to set off early in the afternoon. I felt ashamed not to have yet beheld the orb of joy majestically rising out of the sea, after being told it was one of the greatest curiosities of the place. Therefore I stood on the gallery to witness the magnificent spectacle and I did not return to my chambers until I was nearly blinded by the stream of living gold which hid the surface of the water, when the sun, like a globe of fire elegantly emerged from its watery bed. It is with great regret that I leave Long Branch.*

Victorine DuPont's story is not unlike others who visited Long Branch out of curiosity or for a curative rest by the sea, leaving with their lungs full of salt air and their hearts filled with wonderful memories and stories to tell.

The First Lady Arrives

One visitor to Long Branch is well-known in American history as the wife of President Abraham Lincoln, but she is not as readily identified as the woman who put her official stamp of approval on Long Branch as a place to vacation. It is not certain why Mary Todd Lincoln, her two sons Tad and William, her sister and a group of friends came to Long Branch in the summer of 1861; perhaps it was to escape the oppressive heat of Washington and its polluted Potomac River or the chaos connected with the beginning of the Civil War. Her trip nearly coincided with the battle of Bull Run. The war was just beginning and the new army recruits from Long Branch were drilling on the corner of Broadway and Myrtle Avenues. The soldiers, along with the rest of the town, stopped what they were doing and paid proper homage to the first lady of the land. For the moment, Mary Todd Lincoln was the focus of the day.

Today that visit is only a distant memory, but on August 22, 1861, her arrival did not go unnoticed or unannounced. A *New York Times* reporter was sent to Long Branch to cover every detail of her trip. And of course, all of the local newspaper reporters were in constant correspondence with their editors.

The *Monmouth Inquirer* of Freehold, New Jersey, a weekly newspaper, reported that Mrs. Lincoln's arrival in Long Branch caused much excitement. All along the beach, from every hotel and in every dooryard for miles around, the American flag floated in the breeze and flashed in the sunlight. A number of little girls dressed in white lined the passage from Mrs. Lincoln's railroad car to the carriage, and an immense procession of people followed her from the depot to the hotel.

Mrs. Lincoln chose to stay at the Mansion House Hotel. It was Long Branch's finest hotel and one of the largest at the time. *Frank Leslie's Illustrated Newspaper* printed an article that described the hotel: "Among the fashionable summer hotels of our great Republic, the Mansion House, Long Branch, occupies a prominent position, not only on account of the spaciousness of the building, the airiness and comfort of the rooms, the healthfulness of the spot, and the beauty of the location, but for that genial air of home which the proprietor, Mr. Laird throws over it." Samuel Laird had purchased the hotel in 1852. It was located on the western side of what is now Ocean Avenue and Laird Street.

The local newspaper, the *Long Branch News*, went on to say that there were rumors of all sorts of festivities planned in honor of Mrs. Lincoln and reported, "These are to be so managed and of such a character that they will not interfere with her expressed desire to be quiet and secluded." Her itinerary, according to the *Monmouth Inquirer*, was closely followed. On Saturday she witnessed a cricket match between the Long Branch and the St. George's Clubs, in which the best players of New York and Philadelphia competed.

The *New York Times* reported that Mrs. Lincoln

> *during her brief sojourn at Long Branch, has manifested much interest in that class of its residents who are so famous for their daring exploits as surfmen, of who's heroic efforts in saving the lives of passengers and seamen wrecked upon this exposed part of coast she had heard so much about. She has expressed a desire to be made acquainted with the methods adopted for rescuing the crews of shipwrecked vessels. Ex-Governor William Newell of New Jersey, who is now superintendent of life-saving stations along the coast got up an exhibition which was witnessed with great apparent interest by Mrs. Lincoln and was attended by nearly all those in the town.*

The *New York Herald* reported that Mrs. Lincoln and the excited crowds watched from the beach and bluff in front of the Mansion House, as lifeboats were launched and a simulated rescue took place. A bill was in Congress that would formally create and appropriate funds for a National Lifesaving Service. Newell had introduced the bill. His show of skill was for Mrs. Lincoln's entertainment as well as her influence back in Washington.

In addition to Mrs. Lincoln's daytime activities, a grand hop was planned in her honor. It was perhaps one of the most important events to take place in town to date. The *Times*, in a story filed by a special correspondent dispatched to Long Branch, reported that

> *the arrangements for the "grand hop" which was to take place later in the evening were completed and the expectant guests of the Mansion House are preparing themselves in a quiet way for a time of refined enjoyment which seldom occurs, even at Long Branch. The lowering character of the weather,*

with a slight shower in the morning, has tended to prevent the attendance of many who would have been present. Such a day, however, is far more enjoyable here than a bright sunshine, which is reflected with too disagreeable intensity from the white sand which constitutes the principal sail of this favorite resort. A stiff breeze prevails from the southwest, producing a heavy surf on the beach, which is greatly enjoyed by the bathers who have the courage to venture in.

The *Times* reported that the planned events of the anticipated evening consisted of a display of fireworks at eight o'clock in the evening, upon the green in front of the Mansion House, with patriotic music performed by Dodworth's Regimental Brass Band from New York City. The report described the dining room, which was capable of accommodating four hundred and would be decorated with the American flag and bouquets of evergreens and flowers. The carpet in the drawing room was to be taken up and supper tables set up for the guests. Dancing was scheduled to commence at nine o'clock and continue without intermission until the dancers were tired. The guest list was select. Only one hundred tickets at five dollars each were issued. All the ladies staying at the hotel were invited, and no gentleman without a ticket with his name embossed on it would be admitted. No orders were issued for proper dress, but it was understood that the gentlemen would appear in dress coats, white cravats and white kid gloves. Adding a lighthearted note to the story, the reporter added, "I left mine at home," then proceeded to note, "The supper will be dispensed at midnight. The bill of fare I have not seen, but there are evidences that the repast will fully sustain the reputation of the popular caterer and host of the Mansion House. I notice that a delicate regard to the distinguished guest of the place, or some other motive, has left the entire monopoly of bunting to the Mansion House, which enjoys the sole distinction of an American Flag flying over it." He ended the piece by writing, "I close to secure the train which is just about leaving for New York City." Apparently he was racing back to the city to file his story so that it would appear in the next day's edition.

The ball was a great success. A stream of balloons was set off to announce the start of the evening's festivities. The fireworks that had been arranged had to be cancelled due to a thunderstorm, but everything else went according to plan. The guests began assembling at nine o'clock, but Mrs. Lincoln did not make her grand entrance until ten. She was escorted by former Governor Newell. The *New York Herald* described Mrs. Lincoln as

having a simple wreath of white wild roses in her hair and was dressed with elegance. She wore an elegant robe of white grenadine, with a long flowing train, the bottom of the skirt puffed with quillings of white satin, and the arms and shoulder uncovered, save for an elegant point-lace shawl. She wore a necklace and bracelets of superb pearls, and carried a pearl fan. Beyond all comparison, she was the most richly and completely dressed lady present.

Supper was served just after midnight and included platters of oysters and dishes of ice cream. Mrs. Lincoln left the party soon after, but the dancing continued until three in the morning.

The party's success was confirmed by the *Times*. The paper reported,

The ball which was given last evening by the residents of Long Branch in honor of the wife of the President of the United States, was the great event of the season at this favorite watering-place. There have been frequent reunions and hops here during the season, impromptu affairs; social, familiar, and chatty, which have been enjoyed by the boarders, and the comers and goers at Long Branch but the Grand Hop, which came off last evening excelled in the brilliancy of its appointments, and threw into the shade all previous entertainments of the kind. The "programme" was carried out to the letter and reflected much credit upon the good judgement and refined taste of the planning committee.

Because of the storm, the locals did not venture out in the numbers anticipated. But those who did brave the weather took refuge under the porches and piazzas of the nearby hotels to get a glimpse of the First Lady. A local newspaper reported, "To the credit of the villagers, it should be said that their curiosity was not obtrusive, they generally contented themselves with sidelong glances at the ladies as they passed from their apartments to the ballroom."

The ten-day visit by Mrs. Lincoln, along with the parties and receptions given in her honor, were a great success for all, in particular for the city of Long Branch. After leaving for New York City to do some shopping and to visit her son Robert, who was attending Harvard, she noted that Long Branch was a grand place to visit. Her stamp of approval was bestowed and the town's new image emerged. Besides a place of quiet accommodations and location along the sea, it now had social standing.

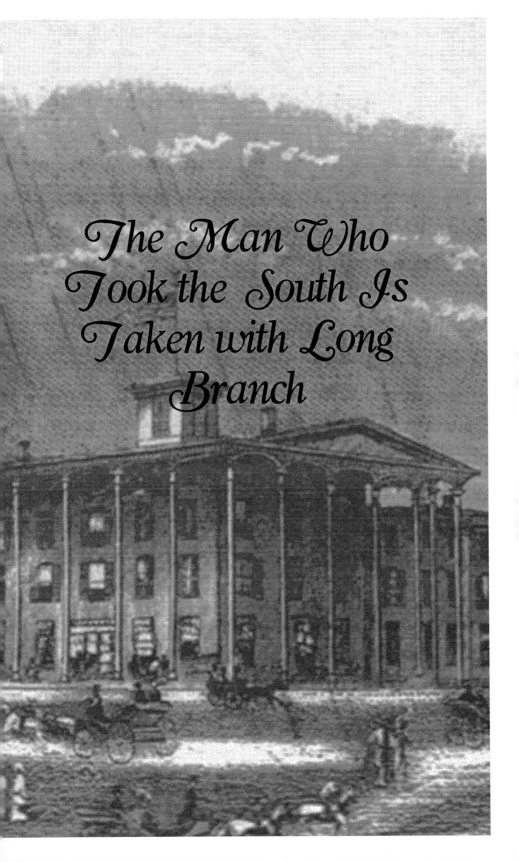

The Man Who Took the South Is Taken with Long Branch

Mary Todd Lincoln always preferred the company of gentlemen. She liked to be the center of attention without the competition that the presence of other females entailed. Historian William S. McFeely writes in his book *Grant: A Biography*,

> *When General Ulysses S. Grant attended a reception at the Lincoln White House, Mary Lincoln was pleased. The new general seemed to her not to be a threat to her husband, and he brought no wife. Wives required either being put in their place if they were attractive, or being made comfortable if they were shy. Since General Grant was alone, Mrs Lincoln could skip wifery and pay full attention to this new second-most important man in the precariously powerful world at the center of which she lived.*

Grant had recently been appointed to the post of lieutenant general of the United States Army. The title carried with it a grand responsibility and a heavy burden: it was Grant's job to win the Civil War. During the evening, Mrs. Lincoln took the opportunity to engage the general in small talk. The two did not always agree on matters of politics, but they often exchanged pleasantries, discussing family and other topics of the day. Perhaps it was during such a conversation that General Grant and Mrs. Lincoln were discussing travel when she told him of her pleasant visit to the seaside resort of Long Branch, New Jersey.

Washington was brutally hot in the summer, and most politicians fled the city and the infestation of mosquitoes that populated the murky Potomac River, causing epidemics of malaria. Some years later, when Grant was deciding where to take his family for the summer, Mrs. Lincoln's words would come to mind.

By the year 1867, the Civil War was over, President Lincoln had been assassinated, and Vice President Andrew Johnson had assumed the presidency.

The Man Who Took the South Is Taken with Long Branch

Mary Todd Lincoln was pleased to meet General Ulysses S. Grant at a reception given at the White House in his honor when he was named commander of the Union Army by her husband, President Abraham Lincoln. *White House Historical Association.*

Ulysses S. Grant was now commander general of the United States Army. In this prestigious position, Grant often found himself in the middle of many heated debates rising from the remnants of the Civil War. One growing controversy was President Johnson's refusal to enforce the Civil Rights Act (the Fourteenth Amendment) of 1866. There was concern among Republicans in Congress about the safety of the freed slaves. As commander of the army, it was Grant's job to appoint northern generals to go south and act as interim governors of individual states. Grant was placed in a difficult situation. President Johnson and Civil War hero, General Philip Sheridan, were at odds over the civil rights issue, according to McFeely:

> *Acrimony was in the air; it was an ideal time for the man caught between the two to take a summer vacation. Long Branch, New Jersey in the 1860s was a lovely seaside village of small houses, true cottages, with wonderful filigreed*

porches from which one could look out from the high bluffs overlooking the Atlantic. The beaches and the surf were fine, and it was here that the Grants spent their summers from 1867 onward.

General Grant chose Long Branch as a place to get away from the controversy brewing between his friend and former comrade, Philip Sheridan and his boss, President Johnson. It was either on Mary Todd Lincoln's earlier recommendation or because several of his most influential friends were already summering in this seaside resort that he came here. George W. Childs, the wealthy publisher of the *Philadelphia Public Ledger*, had a cottage here. His neighbors were George Pullman, owner of the Pullman Palace Car Company, and financiers Anthony Drexel and Moses Taylor. All of these men considered Grant a personal friend.

On their first visit to Long Branch in July of 1867, General Grant and his family, which included his wife, Julia; sons Frederick, Jesse, Ulysses S. Grant Jr.; and daughter, Nellie, stayed at the newly built Stetson Hotel. It was located on the northwest corner of Brighton and Ocean Avenues in the West End section of town. The hotel stood on a site that was formerly a farmhouse. In 1832 the farmhouse was enlarged and named the Lawn House, becoming the first hotel to occupy that location. In 1851 it had a capacity for 175 guests. In 1865 a large three-hundred-room addition was completed. The *Long Branch News* described the building as

Three stories high with four turrets rising from the roof, and in each turret are eight rooms. It is in the form of an L, the short angle facing east, being 250 feet, and the long and main front and entrance 362 feet facing south, making an aggregate length of building and portico 612 feet. There are 250 chambers, twenty private parlors, and there are upwards of forty miles of bell wire distributed through the house. There are gas and bells in every room. There are bathrooms, and every other convenience on every floor, that is to be found in the most fashionable modern hotels.

On June 21, 1866, it was ready for business and the summer season that lay ahead. Under the new ownership of Charles S. Stetson Jr. it was opened as the Stetson House. On opening day the house was almost filled to capacity. In 1867, when the Grants arrived for a quiet family vacation, the Stetson House was one of the most popular hotels in which to stay.

While vacationing in Long Branch, President Johnson summoned Grant back to Washington for a talk. This was July 1867, and the president was not happy with the job that Secretary of War Edwin M. Stanton was doing and wanted to replace

On July 26, 1869, the citizens of Long Branch gave a grand ball in President Grant's honor. It was held at the Stetson Hotel located at the corner of Ocean and Brighton Avenues. Many of Grant's Civil War soldiers were in attendance, including Generals William Tecumseh Sherman, George Meade and Philip Sheridan. *Long Branch Historical Association.*

him with General Grant. Upon returning to Long Branch, Grant responded to the president "tactfully but firmly that such an appointment would break the law," according to McFeely. Now he could enjoy the remainder of the summer season with a clear conscience and the growing respect of the nation. Once again, Grant assumed the role of a thoughtful leader.

Little did he realize to what extent that leadership quality was going to affect his life and the entire country. Two years later, he was voted president of the United States and inaugurated in March 1869.

The following summer, Grant returned to Long Branch not as General Grant, but as President Grant. And this time it was not as a hotel guest, but as a homeowner. His neighbors would be that same group of millionaires who had befriended him many years ago. One of these men, George Childs, recalled Grant as saying, "In all of my travels I have never seen a better place suited for a summer residence than Long Branch." And what a residence he would have!

Wanting the status of having a president of the United States as a neighbor and political playmate, George Childs, Anthony Drexel, George Pullman and Moses Taylor pooled their money and presented the Grant family with a beautiful seaside cottage. It was located at 991 Ocean Avenue in Elberon. To the south of the Grant cottage stood the cottage of Moses Taylor and to the north, the George Childs home. All three structures stood stately on the bluff overlooking the Atlantic Ocean. Anthony Drexel and George Pullman lived a bit to the north on Ocean Avenue.

A cottage in the 1860s was no less a mansion than other fine homes of the day. Because it was meant as a vacation home, a cottage was less formal and blended in with the surrounding area in color and design. Cottagers did not entertain on a grand scale, and the number of servants required to maintain the home was usually less than would be needed in a city dwelling. A cottage was usually built in a location where nature could be enjoyed. At the Grant cottage, natural beauty abounded and the Atlantic Ocean was part of its backyard landscape.

The Grant cottage was built in 1866 for Howard Potter, a wealthy New York banker. The *New York Tribune* called the 2½-story house a mixture of English villa and Swiss chalet and noted that the president and Mrs. Grant often sat on the octagonal porch that faced the street, rocking and watching sightseers passing by on Ocean Avenue. The cottage rested on a grassy bluff that descended to a private beach. There were rope swings in the pine trees for children. It is said that Mrs. Grant always left a jar of cookies on the outside stairs that led directly to the upstairs bedrooms. This was to direct the children away from the front door and to keep their sandy feet from going into the parlor. *Harper's Weekly Magazine* ran a short article entitled "Life at Long Branch," dated September 1876. It described the cottage as

a lovely home; and when the President sits on his back piazza of a summer evening to smoke his after-dinner cigar, with his gentle and amiable wife and his comely children about him, it is a sight which no lover of this country need feel uneasy at seeing. At such a time, doors and windows all wide open, and the interior gives glimpses of a comfortable, but not showy home, with pictures and books about and lamps burning, perhaps a group of carriages will come rolling down the road from the hotel region, and a crowd of friends and fellow citizens, with a band of music, will invade the lawn. Then the family will sit listening, to break into a little ripple of applause now and then, and Mrs Grant, leaning over the piazza rail will chat familiarly with whomsoever chances to be standing near, and press her visitors to come in. "Do come in," I once heard her say on such an occasion, "We can give you a cracker at least in our little kitchen." She is simple, unpretentious, and kindly; a scene like this is typical of her.

President Grant and his family enjoyed the quiet hours spent on the porch at their summer cottage that was located at 991 Ocean Avenue in Elberon. *Author's collection.*

Julia Dent Grant was certainly a woman to be admired for her sweet disposition and quiet determination. She and Ulysses were a good match, mentally as well as physically. There is a legend in the Grant family that one day, while Julia and Ulysses were sitting on the porch at Long Branch, their son, Frederick, also known as Buck, ran out of the house and, ignoring the porch stairs, hopped over the railing. Amused, Grant asked his wife what she would do if there were a fire and the railing ran clear around the porch. Without a word, Julia got up, walked to the railing, grasped it with both hands and vaulted to the ground below.

The cottage at 991 Ocean Avenue in Long Branch would be their summer home for the next fifteen years. Their residence there would give Long Branch the epithet "the Summer Capital."

In the year 1869, besides being the recipients of a lovely home in the city, the Grants were also on the receiving end of many receptions and balls given in their honor. That summer the residents of the city wanted to give them a welcome in the form of a large ball. The Stetson House offered to host the much anticipated event and immersed its staff into the preparations. The date of the ball was going to be July 26. The next day *Harper's Weekly* reported,

It can be imagined what excitement was occasioned by the announcement of a ball at Long Branch, on the evening of July 26 in honor of President Grant. The event took place at the Stetson House, and the entire establishment was devoted to it. It was a grand affair. The President, of course, was there; as was Secretary of the Navy, Adolph Borie, General William Tecumseh Sherman, General Philip Sheridan, and other prominent personages. The grounds around the hotel were illuminated with calcium lights, and the stream of fashion poured endlessly on and emptied itself out at the doors of the Stetson House. President Grant became a martyr, as he has so often done before, and shook hands with about four hundred of the guests. The President retired to a sofa, but General Sheridan took part in every dance. About midnight supper was served on a table 190 feet in length. The most prominent of the guests then retired, but others returned to the festive dance, and kept it up until morning.

With the dateline of Long Branch, New Jersey, and a headline reading "The President's Ball—Large Assemblage of Distinguished Guests," the *Times* reported on its front page,

The grand ball given in honor of President Grant took place at the Stetson House this evening. At ten o'clock the dining rooms were thrown open and Gilmore's Band of Boston and the Governor's Island Band united and played Hail to the Chief. *The President entering with his wife. Distinguished guests from all parts of the country were present. The ballroom was handsomely decorated with American bunting. At eleven o'clock the room was packed to its utmost capacity.*

The night of the ball proved to be sweltering hot, as the humidity that hovered over the oceanfront made the air thick with moisture. President Grant did not like dancing. On a hot night such as this, the sofa was probably his place of choice. In addition to this grand ball, there were many other parties, which he was asked to preside over. To lead the grand march at these events was an ordeal from which Grant would have gladly spared himself. As recorded in the 1940 WPA project *Entertaining a Nation,* "He found even an ordinary waltz or polka too much for him, and at the end of one such attempt on a Long Branch floor, he turned to his partner and confessed, 'Madam, I would rather storm a fort than attempt another dance.'"

Now that Long Branch was known as the Summer Capital, it was set on its course to become the pinnacle of places to see and be seen. Because of President Grant's prominence, other well-known people often visited him here. Many

The Man Who Took the South Is Taken with Long Branch

Stetson House. *Author's collection from Frank Leslie's Illustrated Newspaper.*

times these men of notability were so impressed with Long Branch, they became regular visitors and also purchased homes in the area.

A lesser-known visitor to Grant's summer home in Long Branch was a French sculptor named Frederick Bartholdi, whose most famous work was the Statue of Liberty. He paid Grant a visit in 1871 and told him about his plan to build a monument to America and her role as protector of freedom and abolisher of slavery. Bartholdi said that France would pay for the statue if the United States would fund the pedestal and foundation. While in Long Branch, he asked Grant for his help in securing subscriptions for this fund. Grant was enthusiastic and asked his wealthy acquaintances for their financial help. The Statue of Liberty was meant to be standing in time for America's Centennial, but it was not completed until 1885, a year after Grant's death.

Grant's company was desired by all of the socially, financially and politically powerful people summering in Long Branch, but many times it was the simple workingman whose companionship Grant sought. By nature he was a quiet and unassuming man. It is said that during the Civil War he would rather sit on a tree stump and smoke a cigar with one of his enlisted men than dine with the majors and generals in formality.

In keeping with his humble habits, General Grant rose each morning at seven o'clock and drove along in his buckboard for twenty miles along the oceanfront, passing through the towns north of Long Branch. He and his horses, Egypt and Cincinnati, enjoyed the fast driving conditions along the unpaved stretch of Ocean Avenue. Along with driving his lively bays through town, he enjoyed swimming in the ocean, frequenting the gambling houses, smoking cigars and drinking. Grant also enjoyed chatting with the locals.

According to *Entertaining A Nation*, "He would spend hours swapping yarns with Lem Van Dyke, the special policeman on duty at Grant's cottage, or with Henry Van Brunt, who owned the bathing pavilion opposite the Mansion House in West End." The book notes, "It delighted the local residents to see Grant pull up at the bathing pavilion with his high stepping horses and smart buggy and wait for Henry. Presently Henry would appear with his pants rolled up high above bare, blistered, and sandy feet and get into the carriage and ride up and down the boulevard in the afternoon parade of horse and buggies." The fashionable thing to do at that time was to get dressed up and show off your horses and carriage on a drive down Ocean Avenue. Besides being good company, apparently Henry Van Brunt was the only one in Long Branch who knew how to mix a good drink.

Another local friend of Grant's was the one-legged toll-keeper stationed at Morris and Main Streets. Grant's first meeting with him was far from friendly. Grant was driving down Main Street (now Broadway). Thinking that he would not be asked to pay a toll, he drove straight past the tollhouse. When the gatekeeper hobbled after him to demand payment, Grant said, "Maybe you don't know who I am? I am the President of the United States." The toll-keeper shot back, "I don't care if you're President of Hell, it's your business to pay two cents toll and my business to collect it." Two coppers were promptly paid, and on many days Grant thereafter could be seen sitting and chatting with the old man.

His humanity was appreciated by the workingman as well as by the high and mighty. His influential friend, George Childs, wrote in the newspaper he owned, the *Philadelphia Public Ledger*, an article that depicted those traits in Grant. It was written after Grant's death and entitled "George Childs' Long Branch Neighbor." It read,

During his Presidential terms General Grant acquired a reputation for reticence. But, in point of fact, among his friends and those whom he trusted, he was not more silent than other men and I found him to be a great talker. He never talked for display; never fought his battles over again; never in the faintest degree sought to extol himself, but entered readily into the spirit of the discussion. He brought to every conversation simplicity, sincerity, directness, and common sense. He had a shy wit and had a great appreciation of it in others. He had an endearing way with children and was especially adroit and charming in dealing with his own children. I watched him on many an occasion engage his youngest son in conversation and they always enjoyed each other very much. If the General didn't know you, his conversation was yes, yes, no, no, or maybe. Nobody ever heard him swear, and nobody ever heard from his lips an indelicate or equivocal expression. I spent a long afternoon with him at his seaside villa

The Man Who Took the South Is Taken with Long Branch

at Long Branch a dozen years ago in the company with two of his friends, and his conversation was full of variety and interest.

Some of those interests involved food. During his summers in Long Branch, Grant would often take his horse and buggy and ride over to Pleasure Bay in the north end of town. He liked to visit Price's Hotel. Mrs. Price would fix him his favorite meal of Spanish mackerel. At the time Price's charged four dollars for a shore dinner. He would also frequently stop at the Hollywood Hotel, where he would enjoy a weekly chat with John Hoey, a piece of freshly baked huckleberry pie and a strong drink or two. Hoey was a millionaire. He owned the hotel, a vast amount of property and numerous cottages on Cedar Avenue. He also owned Adams Express, a company that transported millions of dollars worth of gold bullion from the United States Treasury to financial centers throughout the country.

Always one not to shy away from a bet, Grant was a regular at Phil Daly's Gambling House. Here he would gamble, smoke big black cigars and drink whiskey. Some of his political detractors would criticize his habits as well as his governing skills. Grant responded to these comments by saying, "The words of these men roll on as incessantly as the Atlantic Ocean."

In 1870 Monmouth Park Racetrack opened and President Grant had a box seat. The racetrack was located several miles west of Long Branch in Oceanport. The first race was held on the Fourth of July.

Grant continued to summer in Long Branch even after his term as president was over. In his years of retirement he had many financial ups and downs. Bad stock investments, the Black Friday gold market panic and the Whiskey Ring Scandal all had devastating effects on his cash flow. But through it all he continued to hold onto the security of his house in Elberon. The sea air and pleasant atmosphere gave him peace. It was also a place for family to gather. In 1874 his daughter Nellie came from her marital home in England to give birth to her first child in her father's summer cottage on Ocean Avenue.

Suddenly the place of so much enjoyment was the scene of heartbreak. On a summer day in 1884, Grant and his family were sitting in their living room in Elberon. Julia Grant wrote in her *Personal Memoirs,*

There was a plate of delicious peaches on the table of which the General was very fond. Helping himself, he proceeded to eat the dainty morsel; then he started up as if in great pain and exclaimed: "Oh my, I think something has stung me from the peach." He walked up and down the room and out to the piazza and rinsed his throat again and again. He was in great pain and said water hurt him like liquid fire. That was the very beginning of his throat trouble. I also thought it was a sting from some insect in the peach.

Grant was suffering from the first signs of the throat cancer that would bring about his death within a year.

That final year proved to be one of most financially productive ones of his life. He knew he was dying and worried about providing for his family. He started thinking about writing his memoirs and selling them. While sitting on the front porch with his Long Branch neighbor, George Childs, he asked him if he thought anyone would buy a book written by an old army general. With Childs's encouragement he began writing his memoirs and searching for a publisher. Many publishing houses stepped forward but were not fair in their financial offers. The famous writer Mark Twain, also a frequent visitor to New Jersey, stepped forward. He offered to publish the two-volume *Personal Memoirs of U.S. Grant*. It is now considered to be one of the most comprehensive writings on a war experience.

The Elberon cottage was sold in 1884. Through the winter, Grant continued writing his memoirs in New York. The manuscript was completed 106 hours before he died on July 23, 1885.

The Summer Capital

Rutherford B. Hayes succeeded Ulysses Grant when he became the nineteenth president of the United States. In 1876, as Grant was nearing the end of his second term, *Harper's* questioned the status of Long Branch as the Summer Capital, if his successor did not also choose to vacation here. The article stated,

> *It is quite possible that, unless our next president should choose Long Branch as his summer residence also, many years will elapse before the flow of prosperity will lead to the high prices on real estate which formerly prevailed here. Yet the prediction would be childish to intimate that the best days of Long Branch are over. The probability is that this charming resort will grow more and more in favor.*

Fortunately, Long Branch did not have to face that uncertain fate. Grant's successor, President Hayes, came to the resort often enough to preserve its reputation as the Summer Capital. Unlike Grant, Hayes did not own a cottage here. The president and his wife, Lucy, preferred to stay at the Elberon Hotel. It was the newest and most stylish of the shore hotels at the time. Hayes and his wife, who was nicknamed "Lemonade Lucy" because of her aversion to serving alcohol, preferred to receive visitors at the hotel. The Hayes family was much less social and less sought after than the Grants. The most significant contribution they made to Long Branch was their presence and their ability to attract the group of important statesmen who made their way here to confer with the president.

Despite the well-known simplicity of their tastes, in choosing the Elberon Hotel, the Hayes family was plunging itself into the center of the social set who

The Summer Capital

The Elberon Hotel was built in 1866 after a design by the famous architectural firm of McKim, Mead and White. It was owned by Lewis B. Brown, the developer of the section of Long Branch known as Elberon. *Long Branch Historical Association.*

were also summering there. The hotel was emerging as a popular destination for those who liked to drink, smoke and gamble. The Hayes family took no part in any of these entertainments. When they arrived for the summer of 1877, the hotel was only a year old and already had caught on as one of the premier places to stay. The hotel was built by Lewis B. Brown, the developer of the Elberon section of Long Branch. The town was named by using a combination of Brown's initials, L.B., and pronouncing it "El-bron". He planned the hotel, located in the southern end of Long Branch, to look like a country estate. It was a low rambling structure with deep first-floor porches extending onto the lawn from many angles, suggesting an exclusive residence. It was frequented by many well-known people from the worlds of money, power, politics and entertainment. James A. Bailey, the partner of P.T. Barnum of circus fame, was a regular visitor at the hotel.

In a short while, the Elberon Hotel would be the focus of national and international interest. It would be the place former presidents, statesmen, residents and reporters gathered to await hourly updates on President Garfield's fragile health while he was a mortally wounded patient at a nearby cottage.

The Nation's Patient

James Aaron Garfield was the twentieth president of the United States. Like his immediate predecessors, Ulysses S. Grant and Rutherford B. Hayes, he was from Ohio and had fought valiantly in the Civil War. Although these men were not always in agreement, their opinions concurred on certain fundamental things: they loved their country, their politics and their families.

One more thing these men had in common was their love of the Jersey Shore. During their terms in office and as private citizens, all three men brought their families to Long Branch to escape the intense heat that percolated throughout Washington during the summer. They were all content when their wives and children were settled at the shore to enjoy the cool ocean air and healthy recreation it offered. In Garfield's case, his visit to Long Branch in June 1881, involved more than just a summer vacation.

In the spring of 1881, his wife, Lucretia, also known as Crete, was diagnosed with malaria, an infection that was contracted from the mosquitoes swarming around the polluted Potomac River. For months she ran a high fever and was confined to bed. As she began to regain her strength, it was suggested that a visit to Long Branch, New Jersey, would help restore her to good health. The *New York Herald* reported on June 20, 1881, "The quiet and repose which the President sought in coming to Long Branch he has certainly found at the Elberon Hotel. He has not left his quarters for more than a couple of hours, except to attend church." Garfield attended the St. James Summer Chapel located on Ocean Avenue diagonally across the street from the hotel.

Apparently, the soft ocean breezes and the amenities offered at the Elberon Hotel were just what the doctor ordered for Crete's recovery. The piazzas surrounding the hotel were perfect for walking or sitting and enjoying the sounds of the sea. Colonel Jones, the manager of the establishment, made sure that the

Garfield family were sheltered from the prying eyes of the paparazzi, politicians and social callers. The hotel's accommodations were just as pleasant as the design of the building. Management paid the president the respect due his office by hanging out a large silk American flag. It hung over the main entrance of the hotel. The *Herald* reported that it was the first time since the hotel was built that such a thing was done in the Elberon compound.

The *Herald* also noted that President Garfield's visitors were few. Among those he welcomed during his stay in Elberon was his secretary of war, Robert Todd Lincoln, the son of the slain President Abraham Lincoln. Another visitor was General Horace Porter, a resident of Elberon and President Grant's personal secretary. President Grant and his son, Jesse, were regular dinner guests at the Elberon Hotel, which was located a short walk from their Ocean Avenue cottage. They were not regular callers. Grant and Garfield were not on the best of terms, politically speaking.

Garfield's intention was to spend some quiet time with his wife and to see that she was fully recovered from the ravages of malaria. He did not want to be preoccupied with the political squabbles that were seeping out of Washington. At the end of the week, Crete was feeling better, and Garfield had to put the business of being a good husband aside and assume his presidential duties. He called a cabinet meeting in Elberon and afterward hosted a departure reception for the group. Those in attendance were Secretary of State James Blaine, Secretary of War Robert Todd Lincoln, Vice President Chester Arthur, Attorney General Wayne MacVeagh, Postmaster General Thomas James and Secretaries Windon and Kirkwood. Also in attendance at the Elberon that night was former President Grant. He had put aside his disagreement with Garfield and paid him a social visit at the hotel.

On June 27, 1881, a well-rested and contented president returned to Washington to attend to some business matters. When his paperwork was done, he planned on picking up his sons Jimmy and Harry and returning with them to Elberon. There he would join Crete, and the family would travel together to Williams College in Williamstown, Massachusetts. He was going to enroll his sons in the freshman class and partake in the festivities planned for the twenty-fifth anniversary of his college graduation.

His brief stay in Washington was a reminder of why he and so many others sought out the Jersey Shore in the summertime. The weather in the capital was brutally hot and humid.

Maybe it was because of the heat or his anticipation of joining his wife and daughter, Mollie, in Elberon that he arrived in the Sixth Street Station Depot in Washington early on the morning of July 2, 1881. The forty-nine-year-old president was accompanied by Secretary James Blaine. A special car had been added to the 9:30 a.m. northbound train for the president's private use. As the train approached the station, Garfield and Blaine entered the ladies' waiting room on their way to the boarding area. Little did they know that they were being followed by a madman. His name was Charles Julius Guiteau, a political hanger-on who had been following Garfield's movements between New York and Washington since his presidential inauguration in March, hoping to gain an appointment as a foreign diplomat. Garfield and Blaine, arm-in-arm, had taken only a few steps when the sound of a pistol shot was heard and the president gasped, "My God, what is this?" before collapsing.

Two shots from the pistol Mr. Guiteau had been concealing critically wounded the president. Travel plans were reversed and Mrs. Garfield rushed by train from Elberon to Washington to be at her husband's bedside.

Dr. D.W. Bliss, the president's personal surgeon, was immediately called to the White House. Bliss chose a staff of doctors to help treat the "nation's patient." His medical team included Surgeon General of the Army Joseph K. Barnes, the doctor who had assisted in treating President Lincoln when he had been fatally shot by John Wilkes Booth in 1864. Others on the team were Dr. D. Hayes Agnew of Philadelphia and Dr. Frank H. Hamilton of New York City. Garfield's cousin, Dr. Silas Boynton, and a female homeopath, Dr. Susan Edson of Cleveland, were also consulted.

One bullet had grazed Garfield's arm, the other entered his back and lodged above his third rib. The hope of the physicians was to locate the bullet and remove it. To accomplish this, they began prodding and probing, opening and irritating the wound more and more each time. The bullet proved to be elusive, but its effects were obvious. The president grew weaker day by day but still retained all of his mental capacities. When his son Jimmy came to his bedside, Garfield told him not to worry: "Don't be alarmed Jimmy, the upper story is all right, it is only the hull that is a little damaged."

At that time, medical science was not sophisticated. There were no antibiotics to treat infection or X-ray machines to help detect what was going on inside the body. Garfield's doctors were relegated to using primitive methods of exploratory surgery, unwittingly causing infection. Everyone in the country and abroad was hanging onto every medical bulletin coming from the White House because the president's condition was so tenuous.

One concerned citizen was the inventor Alexander Graham Bell. From his laboratory in Boston, he was eagerly seeking news of the president's condition. When he heard that the bullet was still not located, he offered to make the trip to Washington to try out one of his inventions. It was a new apparatus called an induction balance that he was using on Civil War veterans. Bell hoped that passing the device over the president's body would make it ring when it detected the metal bullet. Two attempts on August 1, 1881, failed to locate the assassin's bullet. Bell later learned that Garfield's mattress had steel springs, which caused the device to buzz over an area too widespread to pinpoint any one spot in particular.

As the end of August approached, it was apparent that the president was not getting any better. It was felt by all concerned that the humidity that was hovering over the city was stifling his recuperative powers. Even the patient himself realized this and asked if a change of scenery and climate would be beneficial.

Since Elberon had been the spot that helped restore Crete to health two months earlier, it was decided that the president should have the same opportunity. Dr. Bliss agreed that the sea air would be beneficial, and he urged that the president be removed from Washington as soon as possible.

When it was decided that the Elberon section of Long Branch was to be the destination, many of the local cottage owners offered their homes to be used as a temporary hospital. The cottage that was chosen was owned by Charles Franklyn, an officer of the Cunard Ship Lines. The home that he so graciously put at the president's disposal was a twenty-room residence on the beach in Elberon. It was a typical summer cottage, designed by the famous architect Stanford White, a partner in the McKim, Mead and White architectural firm from New York City. It was part of an exclusive compound, which included the Elberon Hotel and several other cottages, set on a bluff overlooking the ocean. Mrs. Garfield and the president expressed their preference for Long Branch. Mrs. Garfield told a *Times* reporter, "We are informed that the climate is very salubrious and that September and October are especially fine months on that coast. Besides, he can get many comforts and appliances that he can get nowhere else. The house that has been chosen is described as having very large rooms and plenty of them and as being provided with fireplaces and radiators, so that we can regulate the temperature there as well as here."

So Elberon and the Franklyn cottage it was going to be, but a decision needed to be made as to how to get there. Was the fallen president too frail to survive a railroad journey? The *Times* reported on September 3, 1881, that when their correspondent in Washington asked Dr. Bliss about the president's preferred destination, Dr. Bliss replied, "He wants to go to Long Branch and says he prefers to go by rail. He is extremely anxious to get away. The salt air of Long Branch would do him a wonderful amount of good, and the benefit to his morale would be incalculable."

As far as travel arrangements were concerned, a prominent summer resident of Elberon stepped forward to assist in giving the president a comfortable railroad

The Franklyn cottage was the seaside home of Charles Franklyn, president of the Cunard Ship Lines. Located along the ocean in Elberon, it was the site chosen by President Garfield's doctors as the perfect place to bring him to try to heal him after he was mortally wounded by an assassin's bullet in 1881. *Long Branch Historical Association.*

trip. George Pullman, president of the Pullman Palace Car Company would provide the transportation. Dr. Boynton reported, "The President will be out of the White House and on his way to Elberon in five days. At this point, malaria is a far greater threat to his health than the six hour train trip." It was the best news emerging from the sickroom since July 2, the day the president was shot.

President Garfield was eager to leave Washington and his doctors were just as anxious to remove him. They said that the stench from the Potomac flats could be detected in the White House. The odors were permeating every nook and cranny within the entire city of Washington.

The first step of the journey was deciding how to move the president from the White House to the train station depot in Washington. It was suggested that it would be convenient to lay a temporary spur to the main track from the White House to the depot in Washington and, on the other end, build a rail line from the Elberon train station to the cottage.

The initial leg of the trip was to be taken on the Baltimore and Potomac Railroad and the final portion was to be aboard the Pennsylvania Railroad. It was proposed that the locomotive be placed in the rear of the train or to burn anthracite coal so that the president's lungs would not be burdened by the harsh exhaust fumes coming from the engine.

The Nation's Patient

The Pullman car that Mrs. Garfield, family members, selected friends and the doctors would be riding in had a long history of proud service to the United States. The car was used for many years by General Winfield Scott on his long journeys through the southern and western parts of the country at the end of the Mexican War. His war injuries made it difficult to travel. This means of transportation offered him privacy and comfort. It also carried all of the most distinguished guests that the Pennsylvania Railroad management had entertained. Washington dispatches noted that it was held in readiness to carry the wounded president away from the malarial atmosphere of the White House at a moment's notice. Although old, it was one of the finest pieces of workmanship the skilled machinists at the plant in Altoona, Pennsylvania, had ever produced. According to the *Times*

Special tests were performed on the springs, which were made of the finest steel and were eight in number, twice as many as the new Eastlake Coaches have. There are twelve wheels instead of eight, and in the running movement of the coach there is scarcely any perceptible jar, owing in measure to extraordinary stability of the construction. The sides are blood red in color, like most of the Pennsylvania Railroad coaches and absolutely without ornament. Even the usual gold work is conspicuous by its absence. The rest of the car is brown. The wheels are like those used under the Pullman Parlor Cars and are painted a bright green, unlike the other stock of the railroad. The car's number is 120 and is noticeable on account of its unusual length, 63 feet having been found none too long for the builder's notions of what a private hotel car should be. Inside it has a drawing room, private bedroom and bath, dining room and a mahogany table large enough to seat ten people at the same time. The kitchen is furnished in a way that would satisfy the most exacting cook. The platform at one end of the car is five feet wide and enclosed by an iron railing with seats for those who choose to sit in the shelter of the low side windows with the scenic panorama gliding away in the wake of the train for the President's car is the rear one. Signals are exchanged with the engineer by means of an electric bell. The drawing room of the car resembles a cozy cabin of a yacht designed for luxurious sailing. There are books and writing desks, as well as card tables, while over the bookcase a small French clock ticks sharply even when the car is idle. The woodwork of the interior is black walnut. There are soft rugs on the floors and easy chairs near the walls. The drawing room is lighted by eight windows and at night by a middle cluster of four lamps overhead with as many more on the side. The rigid simplicity of the exterior has not been carried out here, for the drawing room is ornamented by solid mahogany and finished in silver and gold. A door on one hand leads to the private room of the President of the Pennsylvania Railroad, and a smaller apartment with sufficient room for a narrow bedstead, not a bunk, which faces two windows on the opposite wall, while a second door leads to the bathroom. From the opposite side of the drawing room a narrow passage way leads to the dining room which is twenty five feet long and about ten feet wide, or the full width of the car. Above the carpet, the finishing is partly in cherry. The divans extending parallel with the dining table are upholstered in golden plush. There are four folding beds overhead constructed on the Pullman pattern, and which have been used by many directors of the Pennsylvania Railroad. In the dining room as in all of the other areas of the car, there are ventilators which may be opened in the opposite direction from which the car is moving, thus ensuring plenty of pure air without causing a current through the car, while the fine wire sieve netting covering ventilators effectively guards against flying cinders and dust. A broad table with square corners stands in the middle of the dining room, while on either side, by pulling back the silk curtains a view is had of the scenery outside. Two folding doors opening from the dining room lead to the kitchen, which is almost as large. It contains a pantry, a large kitchen range with an oven overhead, a broad table, wine cooler, and smaller closet for dishwashing and other culinary operations. All that is visible to the eye in the finishing of the kitchen is solid wood like the rest of the car; the metallic work is of polished brass, after the style of modern yachts. Devoid as the car is of cumbrous furniture or unnecessary weight of any kind, it is still said to be heavier than any of the other coaches belonging to the company. Number 120 was used as a reception car for Colonel Scott after the Mexican War, and the Prince of Wales became the guest of the Pennsylvania Railroad on his extended journey through the southwest. Presidents Grant and Hayes and members of all of their cabinets since 1872 have traveled on this car. The car was placed at the disposal of President Garfield on his journey from his hometown of Mentor, Ohio to the capital before his inauguration just four months ago. It also carried President Hayes away from Washington when his term was over. The refrigerator in the kitchen has ample space for a month's worth of provisions if need be.

When one of the officers of the railroad company was questioned as to the car's readiness to transport the presidential family, he replied that the car was in west Philadelphia and could be ready in half an hour, anytime his physicians decided to remove him. A reporter asked, "What speed will be the most comfortable for the President to travel at?" The officer replied, "That will be up to the physicians to say. There will be an instant communication with

President Garfield's bed was put on a stretcher that was attached to the floor of a specially outfitted railcar. *Harper's Weekly.*

the engineer at all times and the latter will have orders to spend a week on the journey, if necessary."

Now that the principal means of transportation had been decided upon, the details still had to be taken care of. Those details included how to get the president from the White House to the Sixth Street Depot in Washington and then from the train station in Elberon to the Franklyn cottage.

There was much discussion at the White House on the subject of getting the president onto the train that would take him to the Sixth Street Depot. The method was not yet decided upon, but the time and day were: early Tuesday morning, September 5, was the time selected.

The president would ride in car number 268. In Altoona, Pennsylvania, workmen fitted an Eastlake Combination Car by taking out the seats and making room for the contrivance that would hold the patient's bed in place. The car was thoroughly renovated, and a false roof was put in a few inches from the ceiling of the car in order to give the air an opportunity to circulate and keep the interior cool. The partition was taken out and replaced by folding doors, and storm doors were added to the platform. Wire gauze was fastened on the outside of the car, completely enclosing the parlor apartment to keep the car free from dust. The inside was hung with heavy curtains, and thick carpeting was laid on the floor; a bed was also placed in position and mattresses provided. Two large iceboxes were added and filled with ice. One third of the train was set aside for luggage. Forty men worked on readying car number 268, which was finished in seven hours. The outside of the car was painted red and the inside, yellow.

Before putting the patient onboard, the doctors took a trial trip to Bennings Station, not far from the White House, to see how comfortable and non-jarring the ride would be. When some minor adjustments were made, it was declared ready for removing the president to Long Branch.

Mrs. Garfield and daughter, Mollie, would ride in the Pullman Palace Car, along with Colonel Jarvis Rockwell; his wife, Eliza, and daughter, LuLu; Dr. William Boynton; General David Swaim; Private Secretary Joseph Brown; and Colonel Henry Corbin.

Mrs. Garfield wanted the group to be small and select. The Associated Press was not asked to come along on this trip. In order for them to be kept abreast of the president's condition throughout the trip, it was decided that Secretary Brown would obtain medical updates and write out bulletins every half hour. These bulletins would be tossed out the window to waiting members of the press at railroad depots in every town along the way.

The actual removal of the president was scripted beforehand and choreographed to precision. The patient would be carried down the stairs of the executive mansion nearest the West Room. He would be lying in his bed, which would be placed upon a stretcher. The stretcher had arrived at the White House that night. It was made of ash and consisted of two long sidebars with rounded-off ends to be used as handles. Three jointed middle pieces provided with hinges of heavy wrought iron were arranged so that it could be folded. The east stairway was selected because it was the widest in the White House. The president would be borne upon the shoulders of four men who were specially trained to carry him easily. He would be taken out of the front door because in the rear there is an extra flight of steps. A strong platform was constructed from the portico for the purpose of facilitating the bearers in depositing him upon the floor of the vehicle in which he was to be transported to the railroad car.

The vehicle was a large two-horse covered express wagon belonging to Adams Express. It was used for transporting bullion to and from the Treasury Department. John Hoey, a friend of Garfield's from Long Branch owned the company. It was standing in front of the White House and orders were given to the agent of the company to have his horses hitched to it at 5:30 a.m. Dr. Bliss and his staff would be there to inspect it to make sure that the inside of the vehicle was not visible from the outside. Arrangements were made to picket the route with soldiers and policemen so that no person could venture near the gravely ill president. The floor of the wagon was on a level with the floor of the presidential car, which was the principle reason this particular style of vehicle was selected. It would be driven up to one of the side doors of the forward compartment, and the president would be carried into the rear compartment through the double doors and placed in position upon the bed frame.

It was a busy day at the White House. One *Times* reporter noted that with so much preparation, "It seemed as though an entire body of government was about to move in group to Long Branch." Transporting just one man was like moving an entire militia during wartime. And this was a war of sorts—a battle to save a man's life.

Attorney General Wayne MacVeagh and his wife had gone ahead to Elberon to make sure that everything was arranged according to specifications. None of the other members of the cabinet, except those who would be accompanying Mrs. Garfield, was planning on going to Elberon just yet. Two other cottages on the grounds of the Elberon Hotel, in addition to the one owned by Charles Franklyn, were made ready as well. Mrs. Garfield and the members of the household would have the exclusive use of one and another would be used as a makeshift office or anteroom, where visitors would be received and information would be given out by Private Secretary Brown.

In the Elberon section of Long Branch, preparations were being made. The Franklyn cottage was a beehive of activity. Newspaper reports described it as "standing almost directly in the rear of the Elberon Hotel, facing the ocean, only a stone's throw from the water. It is one of the handsomest cottages in the compound. The rooms are large, the ceilings high, and furnishings sumptuous. There are four fireplaces so that there will be no difficulty in keeping up an agreeable temperature, even in the midst of a possible cold front." Just that morning coal and wood were delivered, the latter of the finest and thoroughly seasoned were placed in the cottage, and a fire built to make sure that the chimneys were all working properly. Everything was found to be in perfect order. The *Long Branch News* reported,

> Attached to the cottage is a neat kitchen, supplied with everything needed for food preparation. The range in the kitchen was tested and found to be in good working order. Although connected with the cottage, the kitchen is so arranged that no odor from the cooking can reach the rooms of the cottage proper. It is expected that the President's food will be prepared in the Elberon Hotel, but the kitchen will be a great convenience during the night for Mrs. Garfield.

The two other cottages that would be put to use were owned by L.B. Brown. One was on the compound and was designated to be occupied by the president's physicians and nurses who would dine in the Elberon Hotel. The other stood on the opposite side of Ocean Avenue. It would be used by the president's cabinet and their wives.

With every detail in place, it was decided that at six o'clock on the morning of September 6, the president would begin his journey to Elberon. At ten o'clock the night before, the street gates of the White House were closed. The lights were turned out and everyone went to sleep. It would be the last night President Garfield would spend there.

In Elberon there was nothing left to do but wait for the arrival of the nation's patient—or so its citizens thought. At ten o'clock in the morning the day before the president was to arrive, Mr. Harris, the general manager of the New Jersey Central Railroad, received a telegram from Attorney General MacVeagh asking him to lay a temporary track from the Elberon train station to the Franklyn cottage and to do it in less than twenty-four hours. The distance from the station to the cottage was five-eighths of a mile straight down Lincoln Avenue, across Ocean Avenue onto present-day Garfield Road with a gentle curve to the front entrance.

Surveying instruments were ordered from Jersey City so that the route could be laid out. Track master Murtagh was summoned from Newark and orders for ties and rails were hurriedly sent to Elizabeth Port and Jersey City.

At two o'clock in the afternoon, ground was broken by Mr. Murtagh and twelve railroad hands. An hour later laborers began to arrive from all of the lines of the railroad from Jersey City to Sea Girt, and by nine o'clock that night three hundred skilled railroad builders were hard at work. Murtagh said, "They will have the last spike driven by daylight and the road will be as smooth as a parlor floor."

The *Herald* reported,

> *Elberon was the scene of remarkable activity. The surveyors had laid out the route of the track from the upper switch on the main line, extending it east along Lincoln Avenue to the hotel grounds, where the ties were laid on the turf beside the southern drive about one hundred yards south of the hotel. The sea dashes against the cliff or bluff only forty paces away, and a more picturesque and charming retreat for the sick President cannot be found on the coast. The rails were laid to the very door of the cottage on the side toward the ocean, and a platform was built over the doorstep so that the Presidential coach may be carried from the car into the cottage without disturbing the sufferer.*
>
> *Crowds of ladies and gentlemen from the various hotels and cottages along the shore have visited the scene and watched the laborers. Immense locomotive headlights and hundreds of smaller lamps and lanterns gave light to the workmen. Last evening the moon shone in splendor and the scene where the workmen were laying the track is one that will long be remembered. Hundreds*

of costly equipages flashed in the moonlight, finding their way among dusty farmers' wagons that were hauling iron and ties. Hundreds of ladies in drawing room silks mingled with the bronzed-faced workmen who were pushing to complete their labor of love. Society belles and all the interesting representatives of fashion and wealth at the great watering place of Long Branch looked with admiration on the horny-handed men who were shoveling earth for the benefit of the nation, and for once, if never before, capital and labor agreed. For once the millionaire and the day laborer shook hands across the bondholders' railway tracks.

Bakeries and restaurants stayed open to provide the workmen with food and drink that was carried back and forth by tallyhos. The West End Hotel also sent meals.

Everyone worked together, except one man standing by the side of the road. He refused to lend a hand because he did not agree with Garfield's presidential policies. But when he found out that Garfield was a Mason, like he, he pitched the track with hearty pride.

President Grant was at his home in Elberon and waited anxiously for the arrival of Garfield's train and, of course, his ultimate recovery.

Most of the railroad ties were laid by nine o'clock that evening, and the ringing clash of steel rails, the earnest blows of the spike brigade, the silvery voices of the lady visitors, the hum of the carriage wheels, the glare of one thousand lanterns and signal lights and the voices of the engineers giving directions—all these evidences of activity, along with the roar of the ocean, made the night a memorable one.

Most of the cabinet members were settled in Elberon. Secretaries Blaine, Windom, Kirkwood and Lincoln took rooms at the West End Hotel, where thirty-eight additional telegraph wires were put in the circuit.

At daybreak on September 6, the presidential car arrived at the Sixth Street Station in Washington. It was ready for the most important journey it had ever taken and would carry the most important person of the time a total distance of 228 miles.

At ten o'clock in the morning of September 6, the 3,500-foot temporary spur to the rail line was ready to take the presidential train and its prominent passenger from the Elberon train station to the cottage by the sea.

Upon his arrival at the cottage, Garfield was carried upstairs to his room overlooking the ocean. It was the first time he had been out of his sickroom in seventy days. The *Times* reported,

Elberon train station, where Garfield's train arrived and temporary spurs were driven to make his ride down Lincoln Avenue to the cottage. It burned in the 1980s. *Long Branch Historical Association.*

> *The dearest wish of President Garfield's heart had been gratified, and he is now lying quietly at rest in his room in the Franklyn Cottage at Elberon. The long journey was accomplished with remarkable ease. The train bearing the distinguished patient was seen from the porch of the Elberon Hotel rolling into the station at 1:10 pm and instantly the crowds rushed down the lawn as near to the cottage as the military guards would allow. When the crowds saw a bed being brought into the cottage, they assumed it contained the President and dispersed. As soon as the bed disappeared from sight under the awning, they left. Those who remained saw a stretcher carrying the president covered by a white lamb's wool blanket with red stripes. A damp towel listlessly covered his forehead.*

Newspapers reported that when he was settled in his room he turned his head toward the ocean. The *Herald* noted, "A few schooners were standing in toward the shore with a light breeze that just rippled the water. The pure saline air floated in through the wide open window. It seemed to give the President a new

strength. He drew a long breath, a sigh of satisfaction, and said, 'Thank God, it is good to be here.' He did not want to go to sleep and told his doctors, 'Oh, I like to look at the sea.'"

Within an hour of the patient's arrival, J. Stanley Brown, the president's private secretary, had set up his office across the street on Ocean Avenue and would issue updates to the press who were staying at the hotels along Ocean Avenue. The eyes of the nation were focused on Long Branch that summer of 1881. More than one hundred newspapers throughout the country sent reporters to cover the progress and prognosis of the nation's patient. Journalists and telegraph operators set up headquarters at the West End Hotel, about one half mile north of the Franklyn cottage. An express service was set up to handle the hundreds of messages going back and forth.

Dr. Bliss gave his first medical bulletin of the day from the porch of Secretary Brown's cottage. He said, "If the persistent heat did not let up the President would have to be moved out of his present quarters to some cooler place, possibly to a tent on the lawn overlooking the ocean." He added, "Here in Elberon the doctors are helpless unless the weather is favorable." The only two things in favor of being at "the Branch," as Long Branch was often fondly called, were the absence of malaria and the patient's intense desire to be at the Summer Capital. At one time during the day

Garfield's presidential cabinet met in Elberon to discuss the future of the president's health and that of the country. *Harper's Weekly.*

the thermometer had registered 94 degrees in the president's room and 101 degrees on the shaded piazza below.

Carriage after carriage drove into the grounds of the Elberon compound very early in the morning. Silent men, women and children had come to hear the condition of the patient. Many asked to inspect the cars of the special trains that were positioned like iron guards outside the cottage. A photographer's stand had been set up on the grounds to provide the public with informative images. The photographer, hunched under his black canvas camera-cover, was ready at all times, like a sharpshooter, to take aim at the historic comings and goings and record them for posterity.

The focus of everyone's scrutiny was the Franklyn cottage. At this time the cottage was getting more attention than the White House, Buckingham Palace and the Taj Mahal put together. Many newspapers carried precise details of the home design and layout. The *Herald* wrote,

The Nation's Patient

The architects had accomplished their goal of building for Mr. Franklyn, a seaside home that was comfortable and arranged to take advantage of the views and breezes emanating from the ocean. The exterior of the cottage is simple with the exception of the snuff colored peaked roofs, the gables, and sharply defined balconies and piazzas. The cottage sits back from the main road. The sides of the house are paneled with overhanging shingles. The bright red chimneys are in strong contrast to the rather somber aspect of the lower portion of the house. It is in as quiet a part of Long Branch as could have been desired for the President's recovery. It is some distance in from Ocean Avenue and is surrounded by well kept lawns and flower beds. The only intrusion being the sound of the sea. The drive-way divides the culinary area and servant's part of the cottage from the southern portion of the building. The divide extends through the second story where the kitchen is located. This so the cooking odors do not reach the rest of the house. Going through the entrance to the cottage, just a few feet south of the driveway, a large hall is entered. In this hall or vestibule, which is high and broad there are small tables and a fireplace. The entrance door to this hall is so fashioned that the upper part can be opened while the lower portion remains closed. It is in sections. The library and parlor to the south open into this hall. The dining room and pantry are elevated some feet above the vestibule and form two very roomy apartments. All around the east and south of the building there is a piazza. The hall and the dining room together are about fifty feet wide, extending the entire width of the house. The dining room is heavily paneled with hardwood and cork. The veranda, which extends around the building, faces the sea and directly overlooks the bluff. The second floor of the house contains three bedrooms, the south one being occupied by the President. It is about thirty by twenty five feet with an arched ceiling. The ceiling is about twelve feet high. This is said to be the most comfortable room in the house, and in it the President can receive at all times the full benefit of the ozone-bearing breeze from the sea. There is an uncovered piazza about the room, and on the west side are doors leading to the bath and dressing rooms. There is a covered piazza extending around the building just outside of the dressing room on the south and west. One window in the President's room opens directly upon the sea, and there are three windows on the south side.

The *Herald* was so enthusiastic about the house and its arrangements, it published a detailed architectural diagram of the floor plans. It seemed the perfect place for the president to recover. And for the first few days he did show some improvement. On September 8, the *Times* reported Dr. Bliss as saying,

"The President has every condition of convalescence. The President is much better and there is every reason to believe that he will continue to improve." The reporter reminded Bliss that the hot weather experienced in the previous two days was not helping the patient's condition, and many condemned Long Branch for the president's decline, but today the mild but steady ocean breeze has transformed the seaside into an oasis.

The windows of the sickroom were thrown open and as the breezes gained momentum, so did the President's strides toward recovery. Everyone in the city of Long Branch was spreading the good news. Doctor Boynton commented to a reporter on the president's spirits, "The invigorating sea breeze filled him with delight and the sight of the boundless expanse of smooth water breaking into huge rollers on the sand was one that never seemed to weary him. The continuous roar of the ocean is like sweet music in his ears." He was feeling so well he asked General Swaim if he wanted to play cards. President Garfield indicated that he would no longer need the medical assistance of Mrs. Edson, the female homeopath who had come from Ohio as part of the medical team. She was an older woman with a stout build. It is possible that he was embarrassed to have such a matron taking care of his personal needs. He was feeling so strong on this day he asked for his entire cabinet to assemble in Elberon and confer with him at the cottage.

Garfield kept eating and imbibing fluids, and doctors kept taking his pulse and temperature, while continuing to pick and probe at the open wound. They were still hoping to locate the bullet or at least relieve the pressure that was building up from the increasing infection. At other sites, skin eruptions were festering, the doctors never realizing that each time they inserted their fingers or probes into the president's body they were introducing bacteria and causing more infection. But the president seemed to be responding.

The president continued enjoying the soothing ocean breezes and the pleasant temperature inside the cottage. During the middle of the day the roof of the structure was hosed down to keep the interior cool. It was paradise—a fool's paradise. Everyone hung on each improvement, however slight. The day a reclining chair was brought up to the sickroom, the mood was euphoric. For the first time since he was shot two months before, the president's head was elevated higher than his feet.

On September 11, a report from Long Branch was printed in the *New York Times* relating the conditions of the president and the weather,

Notwithstanding a cold, murky, and thoroughly disagreeable storm, and the fact that Saturdays have generally been blue days for the President, today must

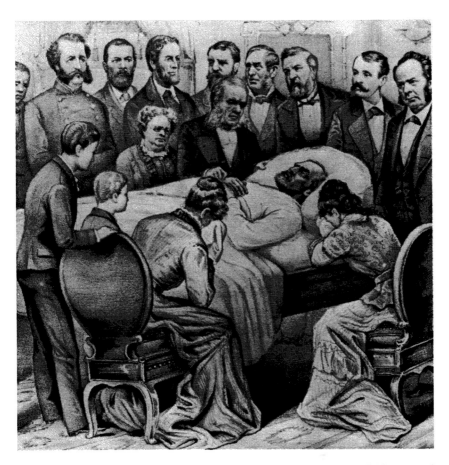

Surrounding President Garfield's deathbed are his cabinet members, medical team and his family. *Author's collection from a Currier and Ives Print.*

be set down as a day of actual and decided progress in the condition of the sufferer at Elberon. The day was ushered in with a thick, sticky fog, which awakened apprehensions in the minds of many timid persons that the effect upon the patient would be anything but good. A drizzling rain began to fall early in the morning and continued until nearly noon. The residents of the Long Branch area were so stricken by the presence of their prominent patient that one local farmer said, "for the sake of the parched and dried-up country, I hope this storm will last a week. We need it, but if it is going to make a hair's weight of difference for President Garfield, I would give my farm to see it stop raining this minute." He expressed the feelings of everyone in town as well as the entire country.

The bad weather did not adversely affect the president, and he continued showing signs of improvement, even though a slight cough was developing. He was feeling much better and wanted to talk business with the members of his cabinet who were hunkered down in various cottages along Ocean Avenue.

The president's recovery was on the mind and in the hearts of everyone from the prominent and powerful right down to the workingman and his family. Two little girls from Pennsylvania heard that the president liked squirrel soup. They sent him their pet squirrel wrapped in a small box in hopes that the broth made from it would make him better. An Alderney cow was delivered from Kelsey's Red Gate Farm in Newton, New Jersey. She was transported in a special car and carefully placed in a stall in the stable connected to the Elberon Hotel. She would graze on the lawn outside the cottage, and local farmers sent in green corn and hay for her to eat. The cow was named Rapartee and she produced twelve quarts of milk a day, which was used for the president's milk punch. He received a tumbler-full every three hours and expressed great appreciation for it. The punches were a mixture of milk with increasing amounts of brandy added each day.

On September 10, 1881, Postmaster General Thomas James ordered that the name of the West End, New Jersey post office be changed to Valley, New Jersey. The West End Post Office was moved into the lobby of the Elberon Hotel to accommodate the huge volume of mail arriving for the president, as well as important incoming correspondence for the cabinet members and officials staying there.

Saturday's visitors to the Elberon Hotel included Secretary of War Robert Lincoln, Attorney General Wayne MacVeagh, General David Swaim and former President Ulysses Grant. Afterward they all dined at John Hoey's cottage on Cedar Avenue. It was the same gracious home at which the president and Mrs. Garfield had been entertained just eleven weeks ago.

The next day all of these men and their wives attended Sunday services at the small seaside chapel across the street from the Franklyn cottage. After a night of pelting rain, the day was exceedingly beautiful. At ten o'clock in the morning, the sky cleared and the sun shone and dried the muddy roadways of the city. A reporter noted,

> *The grass and foliage seemed to be infused with new life and vivid colors. The sea stretched calm and blue for many miles into the clear atmosphere. Small details of distant vessels were distinctly visible to the naked eye. At times myriads of gulls could be seen hovering over schools of blue fish. A southwest*

wind cooled the air to a most enjoyable degree. The walks and verandas were crowded with elegantly dressed ladies and gentlemen and the roads were crowded with handsome equipages. The president apparently felt the influence of his surroundings. He was in lively spirits and talkative. His bed was wheeled to the window and he gazed upon the scene. A sentry on duty was pacing up and down upon the lawn and came within range of the president's vision. He waved his hand as a salute and the soldier instantly stopped, faced front, and presented arms.

On September 12, Secretary of the Navy William H. Hunt came to visit. "Old Salt" and "Old Neptune" were nicknames Garfield had given Hunt. When he entered the sickroom, the naval officer pointed to the ocean and said, "See you had to come to my element to get better." President Garfield replied, "Yes" and waving his hand toward the open window said, "There she is, and it is good."

The surgeons were enjoying their after-breakfast cigars on the porch of the Elberon Hotel when word came that the president wanted to see them. He wanted to use the reclining chair again. When he was settled in it, President Garfield said, "This is good, I think I should have been taken here three weeks ago." The next day he sat watching the ocean for more than an hour. Dr. Bliss, who was never one to shy away from talking to the press, told a reporter, "Bringing him to Long Branch was the thing to do. I do not believe he would have survived if he had remained in Washington."

All this activity was going on while outside the front door of the cottage, the tracks that had been so hastily laid nine days before were still resting stoically, waiting to take the president back to Washington. The men who had labored so hard to lay these tracks were each thanked personally by the Central Railroad of New Jersey. The letters they received commended them for the promptness and fidelity they exhibited when they were asked to work for twenty-four hours without rest.

From grown men to little children, everyone in the United States wanted to do something to help the president get well. During his stay at the "Executive Cottage," as the Franklyn cottage was called, a package arrived for him. It was a night clock—a small token that represented the sorrowful toll the unfolding of these days in Elberon was taking on the country. The attached card read, "With sympathy from five interested children from Boston."

Maybe it was an omen of things to come because on September 15, the weather in Elberon took a turn for the worse. The reports said, "The darkened sea has been lashed into whitecaps as far as the eye could see and the rollers thundered with increasing force upon the beach. A strong gale of wind has blown from the sea all day, rattling doors and windows, bending trees and shrubbery and leveling the tall grass. It has been cold."

On September 16, Dr. Bliss confirmed what many had been suspecting for some time; the president was growing weaker. He had begun hallucinating, his bedsores had stopped healing and the high fever and cough were persistent. Septicaemia, also known as blood poisoning, was taking hold.

The sky was gray, the sea was angry and the rain was relentless. And as the day grew gloomier, so did the news from the sickroom. Members of the presidential cabinet took turns sitting with the patient, taking round-the-clock shifts.

On September 17, Dr. Bliss entered the cottage of Secretary J. Stanley Brown where he was confronted by scores of reporters waiting to be briefed on the president's prognosis. The doctor found it hard to be encouraging. Back in Washington, special telegrams sent from Long Branch were displayed in the store windows and extra editions of newspapers were issued. Attorney General MacVeagh said that he was glad all of the cabinet members were in Long Branch at this crucial time.

For the next twenty-four hours the president remained in stable condition. The doctors speculated that the low barometer, which had prevailed in Elberon for the past three days, had not helped the situation. Dark and gloomy weather can have a depressing effect on a healthy man, and it was naturally more devastating on a man in the president's condition who had lain upon his back for a total of eleven weeks.

Attorney General Wayne MacVeagh called for a meeting of all of the members of the cabinet. Vice President Chester A. Arthur walked to the Elberon Hotel from his summer home, located nearby on the southwest corner of Park and Elberon Avenues. These men needed to know what the doctors thought the future would hold for them and for the nation.

For a short time, the future looked promising. On September 18, Dr. Hamilton signed the morning medical report and returned to New York, feeling optimistic. Former President Ulysses S. Grant and his son, Frederick, passed through the Elberon Hotel and crossed the lawn separating the hotel from the Franklyn cottage. They were going to visit the patient. The *Long Branch News* reported Grant "looked sad and thoughtful as he passed the people assembled on the verandas." Secretaries Windom and Hunt were at the cottage and greeted him with good news from the sickroom: the patient was feeling better. Grant was relieved and began walking the short distance north to his home on Ocean Avenue. A *New York Times* correspondent asked him what he had learned and Grant replied, "What they tell me today is of a much more reassuring character than I dared to hope for last night." Presidents Garfield and Grant had often disagreed, and this time

Garfield was to prove Grant's assessment of the situation wrong. On September 19, 1881, James Garfield passed away in Elberon, New Jersey.

On that day, from early morning on, the feeling seemed to prevail that the end was approaching for Elberon's honored guest. At the telegraph office, the monotonous click of the instrument bespoke the anxiety of the country with the uninterrupted string of inquiries bombarding it. Men who were engaged in great business interests, politicians throughout the land and representatives of foreign countries all had agents stationed in Elberon to gather information on the president's condition. From all parts of Long Branch, there was a constant buzzing of nervous men clustered in groups, waiting for the outcome that would so greatly affect the future.

That night, at ten minutes to eleven o'clock, word came. James A. Garfield had succumbed to the assassin's bullet. The Elberon saw a scene of excitement it had never before witnessed. Away went coaches and vehicles of every kind along Ocean Avenue. Horses driven at top speed galloped along, messengers on foot raced alongside one another and the whole cavalcade swept north to hotels and telegraph stations to speed away the tidings of the nation's loss. West End was in an uproar and the village was awakened from its night's sleep by the dreary tolling of church bells ringing out the knell of death. Many flocked to the scene at the Franklyn cottage.

In the state of New Jersey, the coroner is empowered and required to hold an inquest as to the exact cause of death. In Monmouth County, where the president's death occurred, there were three coroners. Mr. Eugene Britton was the coroner for Elberon, and a postmortem examination was in keeping with the law.

Two hours after the president's death, Attorney General MacVeagh advised that the President's remains would be in charge of the village undertaker, Clifton L. Morris. An autopsy had to be performed before the body left Long Branch.

The following article appeared in the *New York Times*, dated September 20, 1881:

When the sun appeared this morning the sea was almost still and as the day advanced, the air became hazy and the weather warm. The cottage in which the dead body of the President lay was isolated by pacing guards to whose guns bayonets were fastened. The porch in the rear of the Elberon Hotel was soon crowded with people who gazed across the lawn to the Franklyn Cottage. Carriages were continually arriving and departing in front, and the office of the hotel was still used by correspondents, although the single wire was still reserved for the Governor of New Jersey. The improvised railway track over which the President had been brought to the chamber had never left. It still curved from the roadway across the lawn. It could no longer serve the suffering man who it had borne on his way to the sea. Ex-President Grant came through the Elberon Hotel and walked across the lawn to join the new President of the United States, Chester Arthur, who had been sworn in just hours before. Residents of Elberon watched as the two men entered the cottage together to pay their final respects.

The autopsy report stated the president had died from a heart attack induced by blood poisoning. It also revealed that the bullet wound, which was originally three inches long, had stretched to twenty inches at the time of death. Speculation was that the bullet probably would not have caused too much trouble if it had been left alone.

The casket arrived in Elberon on September 21. It was covered in black cloth and ornamented with solid silver handles and a simple name plate. The Long Branch citizenry were invited to the Franklyn cottage to take a last look at the president. They were admitted from nine o'clock to nine-thirty in the morning. The train bearing the president's body would leave Elberon at ten o'clock.

The *Long Branch News* printed what it was like in Elberon that morning:

A cloudless sky, a clear atmosphere, and a cool breeze from the ocean ushered in the morning. The "Branch" never looked more beautiful. Until 7 o'clock am, the scene at Elberon was one of most profound quiet. Only the uniformed guards slowly pacing through the grass surrounding the cottage gave signs that there was life about. A crowd began gathering outside the cottage and kept increasing. The guard was doubled. Carriages began to arrive and their occupants gathered on the hotel porch. Servants and undertakers' assistants came in and out of the cottage. At 8 o'clock, between four hundred and five hundred persons in holiday attire had assembled on the grass in a long, dense line, close up to the outermost sentries. The roadway bordering the hotel grounds was packed with vehicles. All the faces were sad and respectful. Among the crowd were many country people, farmers and fishermen, and their wives. One of these; a lanky, ungainly Jerseyman, in ill-fitting store bought clothes with long faded locks, a consumptive bend to his shoulder, and a thin goatee that stuck forward almost horizontally half a dozen inches from his pointed chin sauntered aimlessly into the hotel office. In one corner, upon an easel stood a large, framed steel portrait of the dead President. It was heavily draped in black. After a while this attracted the attention of the man. Instantly his slouched hat came off, and approaching reverently, he gazed upon the picture for a few moments. Then noticing that several flies had settled upon the glass, he took out a large handkerchief from his coattail and whisked them away. For fifteen minutes he stood there, like a sentinel, protecting the President's picture from the flies. His demeanor was simple and somber when he turned away with moistened eyes.

At 8:43 a.m., a signal was given that the local people could come forward to pay their last respects to the president. Instantly they began to stream forward, squeezing into the cottage, between files of soldiers. The casket had been placed upon a bier in the center of the room leading off the veranda. It was a plain room with carpeting on the floor and chintz curtains on the windows. The furniture had all been removed and the blinds were closed. A soldier stood guard at each end of the coffin, which had no lid so that the head and chest of the president was on view. Two crossed palm leaves were laid on the lower half of the casket. There were no other flowers. As the mourners arrived they divided into two lines and exited through a door leading to the ocean. For one hour the crowd poured past.

President Garfield's cabinet arrived at 9:30 a.m. At Mrs. Garfield's request, Reverend Charles Young of Long Branch held a short service.

In the meantime, the funeral train had backed up around the curve of the temporary track until the side door of the second of the four cars was directly opposite the cottage balcony fronting the sea. It was covered in black. All of the other cars of the train were also covered in black, including the one that had so carefully carried the President to the sea fourteen days ago.

The train was taking him back to Washington, then back to his home state of Ohio. At 10:01 a.m., it turned slowly from the Franklyn cottage, then down Lincoln Avenue to the Elberon train station. At the same time, St. James Chapel tolled it bells and all men's hats were lowered in a moment of silence. Engine 658 was fastened to the train. The same engineer, conductor and crew were ready to make another trip with the president aboard. As the train pulled out, local spectators lined the tracks. At 10:12 a.m., the conductor signaled, "All right," and the train began its melancholy trip back to Washington, D.C. The *New York Times* reported, "The train which bore the nation's leader so tenderly away to the sea, and with him the hopes of millions of people, has returned, shrouded with symbols of sorrow and burdened with the shape of clay from which the spirit fled in the night in Elberon, New Jersey."

Seven Presidents

Although Chester A. Arthur owned a home in Elberon at the time of President Garfield's death, he was in New York City. It was there that he took the oath of office as the twenty-first president of the United States, returning quickly to Elberon to take his place as the new leader of the country and to escort Garfield's body back to Washington.

Throughout his term as president, Arthur continued to summer in Long Branch. He was a frequent visitor at Phil Daly's Pennsylvania Club, a famous casino in the West End section of town. President Arthur had a knack for enjoying himself. Every summer, he ran the country while still managing to maintain his reputation as a sport and a dandy. He was often seen dining, drinking and smoking cigars in many of the fine hotels that dotted the shoreline. He boasted that he was the best-dressed man to become president, and he fit in well with the rich and famous people populating the city. He could also be seen in his Sunday finery while worshiping at the St. James Chapel, located just around the corner from his Elberon home. Arthur was the first president to drive an automobile.

President Benjamin Harrison summered in Long Branch at the home of a friend, but did not partake in many of the social activities. President McKinley also spent summers at the shore. Neither of these men was as noticed or sought after as his predecessors had been. The main reason McKinley came to Long Branch in the summer of 1899 was to visit Vice President Garret A. Hobart.

Garret Augustus Hobart was born in 1844 at 835 Broadway in a rented house on the western end of Long Branch. He spent his childhood in the town attending the school where his father taught, and he was often seen at the Morford and Company General Store, also located on Broadway. His family eventually moved to Marlboro, New Jersey, where his father opened a general

64

Chester Arthur takes the oath of office. *Author's collection.*

store. Hobart studied law at Rutgers University, and in 1897 became the second United States vice president to be born in New Jersey (the first being Aaron Burr). While serving with McKinley, Garret Hobart became ill. He returned to his birthplace to try to gain strength, as others before him had done, from the fresh ocean air and pleasant surroundings. Normanhurst, the home of Norman Munroe, who had made millions selling dime-store novels, was offered to Hobart as a place to recuperate.

Vice President Garret Hobart and President William McKinley in conversation at the home of Norman Munro, owner of Normanhurst, on the corner of Cedar and Norwood Avenues. *Author's collection.*

Unfortunately, his heart condition did not improve and he returned to his home in Paterson, New Jersey. He died in 1899. On February 1, 1901, the *Long Branch Daily Record* reported that at the time of his death, Hobart owned considerable property in Long Branch. His estate was believed to be worth nearly $2 million, some of it subject to a city tax. Between 1880 and 1887, he had acquired a good deal of valuable oceanfront property.

When Hobart passed away, Theodore Roosevelt assumed the position of vice president of the United States. When McKinley was assassinated in 1901, Roosevelt became the twenty-fourth president of the United States, the position Hobart would have attained if he had lived.

As the country entered into the second decade of the twentieth century, the economy began to droop and Long Branch's reputation sagged along with it. It had not been known as the Summer Capital since McKinley's term as president. Gambling was illegal, and Monmouth Park Racetrack was closed. The city was becoming more a town of workers than socialites. In 1905 the city's principal industry was ice harvesting.

In 1916 Woodrow Wilson revived Long Branch's reputation, and it was once again known to the world as the Summer Capital. Wilson was president of the

Shadow Lawn. *Long Branch Historical Association.*

United States and wanted to run for a second term. He had been president of Princeton University and decided it would be good to return to his native New Jersey to wage his campaign for renomination. An estate named Shadow Lawn was chosen as Wilson's summer White House. It stood on the southwest corner of Norwood and Cedar Avenues, the dividing line between what is now West Long Branch and Long Branch. Datelines on the president's activities always read Long Branch, and Wilson always referred to Shadow Lawn as "our residence at the Branch."

Shadow Lawn was originally owned by John McCall, president of the New York Life Insurance Company. In July 1903, the *Daily Record* reported that McCall had built a handsome countryseat on sixty-five acres of land. The estate consisted of three parcels of land on which an elaborate three-story wood mansion rested majestically on a grassy knoll. It contained fifty-two rooms and had gold-plated plumbing throughout.

When McCall was charged with embezzlement, the house was sold. As the new owner, Captain J.B. Greenut—a Civil War hero and millionaire businessman— was proud to invite the president and his politicos to summer there.

It was from this house that Wilson did his political planning with the many Washington officials who formed a steady stream to Long Branch. Crowds of people came to town hoping to catch a glimpse of President Wilson. September 1, 1916, was Notification Day, and Wilson was officially renominated by his party to run for a second term. Most of the leading Democrats of the day descended on Shadow Lawn to hear Wilson make his acceptance speech.

Woodrow Wilson accepts his party's nomination to run for a second term as president of the United States from the porch of Shadow Lawn. *Long Branch Historical Association.*

Throughout October, special days were designated for supporters from around the country to come to Shadow Lawn to hear the president speak. The estate and the town of Long Branch were in the political spotlight. It was a crucial time. America's position on neutrality during World War I was in question. Theodore Roosevelt wrote a poem criticizing Wilson's policies called "The Shadows of Shadow Lawn," after the very place where Wilson was campaigning.

On election day, President and Mrs. Wilson drove to Princeton, their hometown, to cast their votes and returned quickly to Long Branch to await the results. When Wilson went to bed that night at Shadow Lawn, he thought he had lost the election. His daughter, Margaret, was eager the next morning to tell him it was a mistake; he had won the election and would serve as president of the United States for a second term.

A bill was sponsored to present Shadow Lawn to the government to be used officially as the summer White House. The bill was not passed and the home was eventually purchased by Hubert T. Parsons, the president of W.F. Woolworth Company for $800,000.

A typical scene along Broadway in Long Branch in 1916. *Author's collection.*

The estate Shadow Lawn became known as the summer White House during the time President Woodrow Wilson spent there while campaigning for a second term as president of the United States. *Long Branch Historical Association.*

The Parsons Estate was built by Hubert T. Parsons, president of F.W. Woolworth Company, though he eventually lost it to foreclosure. *Author's collection.*

Shadow Lawn burned to the ground in 1927. Parsons built another Shadow Lawn on the grounds. It was a 130-room marble mansion. Parsons and his wife and sister-in-law lived there in near seclusion until he lost it to foreclosure. Shadow Lawn is now the home to Wilson Hall, the administration building of Monmouth University.

In all, seven United States presidents either summered or owned homes in Long Branch. During their respective terms, all of them worshiped at St. James Chapel. Because of this distinction, it has been given the name Church of the Seven Presidents. Presidents Grant, Garfield, Hayes, Arthur, Harrison, McKinley and Wilson all attended services there.

The Church of the Seven Presidents was an offshoot of the larger St. James Church, which was located in the middle of Long Branch on Broadway. Some, but not all, of these seven presidents attended church there as well. According to *Schenk's Guide to Long Branch*, President Garfield and his family visited the church on Broadway in the summer of 1881. At one of these services, Charles Guiteau

waited outside and was going to fire a shot though the window at the president. Mrs. Garfield got in the way and the plan was thwarted. As history recalls, he succeeded in shooting the president later that summer. During these months the would-be assassin was wandering freely between New York and Washington, floating in and out of public forums hoping to run into politicians who might give him a job.

The Church of the Seven Presidents, which is located on Ocean Avenue, was built in 1879 as a convenience by the wealthy residents of the Elberon section of Long Branch. They did not want to take the long carriage ride to St. James Church on the other end of town. In 1886 the collective worth of the congregation of this small chapel was estimated at nearly $250 million.

When President Garfield was dying at the Franklyn cottage, the bells from the chapel rang regularly.

This chapel is now on the list of National Historic Sites and the National Trust for Historic Preservation. It was used as a museum for many years and is now being refurbished to its former simple beauty. It is one of the last tangible links to Long Branch and its famous visitors.

The Muster Roll

President Grant's presence in Long Branch attracted many noted military leaders to the town. Civil War heroes were aplenty. Their names and ranks included Major Generals George Meade, George McClellan, William Tecumseh Sherman, Phillip Sheridan and Admiral David Farragut. These men came to be in the company of their former commander. Others came seeking political appointments and some simply visited to swap stories while smoking cigars and drinking whiskey on a hotel porch overlooking the ocean.

General Winfield Scott, the Mexican War hero, summered in Long Branch for twenty years. He was known as Old Fuss and Feathers because of his love for military procedure and gaudy uniforms. He ran unsuccessfully for president of the United States against Grant and was a valued confidant to President Lincoln during the Civil War. He was injured in battle during the Mexican War and found it hard to travel. Long Branch resident George Pullman kindly lent him one of his famous Pullman Palace Cars to use as a hotel on wheels whenever he made trips to the Southwest for military reasons.

All of these men are well known for their heroism in war. Another Long Branch resident was equal in importance, but not always remembered; his name was Brigadier General Horace Porter.

As the *New York Times* reported at the time of his funeral on June 3, 1921,

> *A bugler sounded taps over the body of General Horace Porter, the last survivor of the staff of General Ulysses S. Grant, yesterday morning at the Fifth Avenue Presbyterian Church, where leaders of the city's and nation's affairs and representatives of the Army, Navy, and Diplomatic Corps gathered to pay their respects. Few funerals in recent years have occasioned such a large gathering of prominent men... The body of the famous Civil War veteran,*

General Robert E. Lee, who surrendered to General Grant at Appomattox. *Durnell Collection.*

Horace Porter at Appomattox. *White House Historical Association.*

former Ambassador to France, author, orator, inventor and railroad president was taken from the church to the Pennsylvania Railroad Station, where it was placed aboard the 11:55 am train and taken to Elberon, New Jersey. There it will rest in the Porter vault until the General's only daughter arrives from Switzerland and arranges for internment.

The *Long Branch Daily Record* reported that the body reached Long Branch at 1:24 p.m. and was met by funeral director Clifton L. Morris and taken to a vault in Greenlawn Cemetery in West Long Branch. When his daughter arrived from Switzerland, she buried her father in the Methodist cemetery on Locust Avenue in West Long Branch, next to his wife and three sons.

Horace Porter's body was brought to Long Branch because he had resided there for many years. His home in the Elberon section of town was located on the west side of Ocean Avenue between Park and Lincoln Avenues, not far from President Grant's summer cottage.

Porter's ties to Long Branch began when he came here as President Grant's private secretary. He gained this position through many years of valiant service to Grant while he was general of the Union forces. He was at Grant's side at Appomattox when Lee surrendered. While Grant was secretary of war, Porter served as his personal secretary. General Porter resigned from the army in 1873, at the end of Grant's first term as president. He went on to have an illustrious civilian career as president of the Pullman Palace Car Company and inventor of the ticket punch system used in the New York subway system. While serving as ambassador to France, Porter made it his mission to locate and return the body of naval hero John Paul Jones to the United States. He accomplished this at his own expense, and the remains of John Paul Jones now rest in a tomb at the United States Naval Academy in Maryland.

The grave of Brigadier General Horace Porter received a military dedication and marker for being a Medal of Honor recipient. The ceremony was performed at the Old First Methodist Cemetery in West Long Branch, on September 25, 2005.

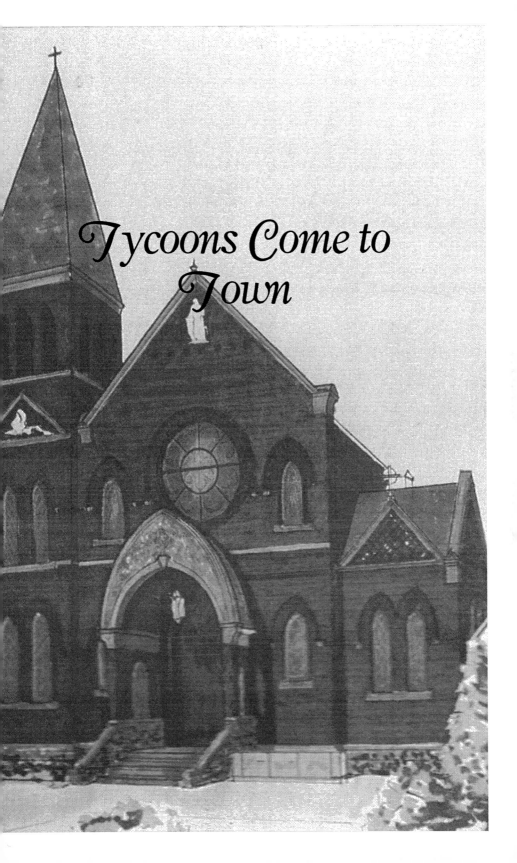

Tycoons Come to Town

The post–Civil War era in America was a time of growth, socially and economically. Industrialization was on the rise, people were on the move and railroads were growing at a pace to keep up with both. Manufacturing and transportation were the businesses to be in. To invest all of this newly made cash, banking was another burgeoning business. The country was growing and so were the pocketbooks of businessmen. Many of them became the nouveau riche, and most of them came to Long Branch to spend their money. They also came to hobnob with the powerful politicians and military bigwigs who were already making Long Branch their summer headquarters. The influence that the new business leaders enjoyed was evident in the political as well as the economic arenas.

These business tycoons became the new arbiters of taste and culture, and the beautiful location of Long Branch fit into their idea of how the wealthy should live. In the late 1800s, there was so much money concentrated in the area during the summertime, a branch of the New York Stock Exchange was set up on the ground floor of the Rothenberg Hotel, which stood on the corner of West End Court and Ocean Avenues. In these golden years, Long Branch was the perfect place to socialize, do business and show off what money could buy.

One of the more flamboyant of these millionaires was James Buchanan Brady, also known as Diamond Jim. He had made his fortune selling railroad equipment and got his nickname because of the number of flashy diamonds he wore. He once boasted that he had a different set of jewelry for every day of the month. Besides his jewelry, he liked to show off his girlfriend, the famous actress Lillian Russell. The pair could often be seen strolling through the hotels or riding down Ocean Avenue in one of Diamond Jim's new "horseless carriages." He purchased six automobiles and hired six chauffeurs, one for each car. The most magnificent

Diamond Jim Brady made his fortune outfitting railroads and spent much of it on jewelry and flashy cars and his girlfriend, Lillian Russell. *Pat Curley Schneider.*

of the fleet was shipped from New York to Long Branch every summer. It had a glass front and was lit from the inside with hundreds of small lights. This was done so that when he rode down Ocean Avenue with Lillian Russell seated next to him, the handsome couple would be illuminated for all to admire. Diamond Jim Brady did not own a home in Long Branch, but was a regular at the best hotels in town and the newly opened Monmouth Park Racetrack. When he died he left his fortune to New York Hospital and Johns Hopkins University.

Art collector and department store mogul James A. Hearn also enjoyed coming to Long Branch. In the 1890s, he built an impressive estate on the corner of Bath and Second Avenues. He loved to entertain. To accommodate his many visitors, he built a special guesthouse adjacent to his mansion. The guest cottage was modeled after William Shakespeare's home on Stratford-on-Avon in England. It was an exact replica of the home of the famous bard. To ensure authenticity, Hearn sent an architect to England to get precise measurements and details of the home Shakespeare occupied in the sixteenth century. In the structure known as the "Shakespeare House," he hung his priceless art treasures. Today these pieces compose the James A. Hearn Collection in the Metropolitan Museum of Art in New York City.

George Pullman was another millionaire to grace the city. In the 1870s he built a large home on Ocean Avenue and others in town for his children. One of the smaller ones still sits on a street in Long Branch named Pullman Avenue. His home was on Ocean Avenue, near President Grant's summer cottage. It was Pullman and several other local businessmen who had purchased the home for Grant in 1869.

Pullman made his money as inventor and owner of the Pullman Palace Car Company. It provided luxurious rail travel to the wealthy. Pullman cars had dining and sleeping areas and were so well outfitted that often they were placed along the sides of railroad yards and used as temporary hotel rooms. The actress Lily Langtry often used one when she was appearing in Long Branch. Her Pullman car was usually parked next to the tracks running through Bath Avenue. These Pullman cars were also used for historic events. One was used to carry President Lincoln's body from Washington to Springfield, Illinois, and President Garfield's family from Washington to Elberon after he was shot.

The Pullman Palace Car Company was so prosperous that Andrew Carnegie saw fit to become its largest investor. Robert Todd Lincoln, son of the slain president Abraham Lincoln, became one of the company's presidents.

Two other important businessmen were neighbors of Grant and Pullman. These men were George Childs and Moses Taylor. One lived on the north side of Grant and the other on the south, both along the bluffs on Ocean Avenue. George Childs was the owner of the *Philadelphia Public Ledger.* Moses Taylor was a New York City financier. President Grant spent many a day sitting on their front porches discussing business and politics. The Taylor home is no longer there, but a church that was built in his honor still holds a prominent place on Park Avenue. It is known as the Moses Taylor Memorial Church. George Childs's home is now a religious retreat house on Ocean Avenue known as Stella Maris.

In addition to Childs, Taylor and Pullman, another local businessman who helped raise the money to present President Grant with his seaside cottage was Anthony Drexel from Philadelphia. His home was located in the West End section of Long Branch right on the brink of the bluffs. He was noted for his wealth, but his cousin Francis Drexel would come to be known for something more than being a millionaire businessman.

Francis Drexel had a home in Long Branch named Sea Cliff Cottage. He also had a daughter named Katharine. As a young girl she entered the convent in Philadelphia. She founded the Sisters of the Blessed Sacrament and donated

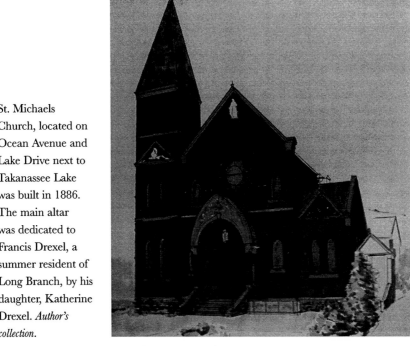

St. Michaels Church, located on Ocean Avenue and Lake Drive next to Takanassee Lake was built in 1886. The main altar was dedicated to Francis Drexel, a summer resident of Long Branch, by his daughter, Katherine Drexel. *Author's collection.*

her entire fortune to this religious order. In Long Branch, she purchased the main altar at St. Michael's Roman Catholic Church and presented it to the church in her father's memory. St. Michael's is the easily recognized red church located on Ocean Avenue, overlooking Takanassee Lake. In 2000 Mother Katharine Drexel was canonized by Pope John Paul II.

Another moneymaker who created quite a stir in Long Branch was Jim Fisk, also known as Jubilee Jim. In the late 1860s he formed a partnership with another millionaire, Jay Gould. Gould had made his fortune in the shipping and railroad business. Their goal was to buy up railroads and manipulate the stock market with their monopoly. Together they made a fortune and spent a great deal of it in Long Branch.

Jim Fisk was a social climber, who was a bit uneasy with his newfound wealth as owner of the Erie Railroad. He wanted to be accepted by the establishment at whatever it would cost. In those days, one way to be noticed was to have a military title, so he bought one. He purchased the bankrupt Ninth Regiment of New York, and with it the title of colonel. He revived the company by offering cash prizes for new enlistments. He often brought the regiment to Long Branch to hold encampments and

The Hollywood Hotel, named for the groves of holly trees that grew on the property, was located on the south side of Cedar Avenue, stretching east to Ocean Avenue. It was built by the millionaire John Hoey in an English cottage house design. *Author's collection.*

entertain the residents. Their duties included performing for military balls, torchlight parades and shooting exhibitions. His campgrounds, named Camp Gould after his good friend Jay Gould, were located on the east side of Ocean Avenue between Broadway and Cooper Avenue. His parade grounds were on Chelsea Avenue. President Grant enjoyed the performances. He would drive up wearing his linen duster, step down from his buckboard and stand next to Colonel Fisk to review the maneuvers.

Fisk and Gould loved Long Branch and couldn't resist combining business and pleasure there. In 1872 they built the Grand Excursion House facing the oceanfront. It had a pier in front of it and train tracks running into a court in the rear. The pier was called the East End Excursion Pavilion. Unfortunately, its instability outdid its lavishness. Within a week of its construction, the wooden structure was washed away in a summer storm. Fisk had hoped to dock his fleet of luxurious steamships there. The *Plymouth Rock* was the most famous of these vessels. It docked on the pier just once before its collapse. This steamship was a floating palace with thirty-two suites and a dining room that housed fifty canaries, perched in gilded cages. Each bird was named in honor of Fisk's special friends such as Jay Gould, Commodore Cornelius Vanderbilt and President Grant.

Another venture of the pair that collapsed was their plan to corner the gold market. Their venture failed, causing the Black Friday panic of 1869. This was a financial disaster that cast a shadow of suspicion on many of the nation's most important men. President Grant was one of the investors involved.

A young gold digger named Josie Mansfield would prove Fisk's final undoing. Fisk and Edward Stokes, the son of a prominent hotel owner in town, were both vying for her attention. After three years of arguments and fights, Stokes shot Fisk dead. Josie Mansfield left Long Branch for Boston where she became a social outcast.

John Hoey, owner of Adams Express Company, built a grand estate on Cedar Avenue that included a mansion, several cottages and the Hollywood Hotel. President Grant often stopped there for a piece of pie or a stiff drink. Hoey's transportation company was responsible for carrying billions of dollars of bullion leaving the United States Treasury. John Hoey entertained many of the most prominent at his establishment in Long Branch. When Oscar Wilde was on tour in America in 1882 he stopped at the Hollywood Hotel before going to visit President Grant.

More money and more people than can be counted spent summers here. One way to measure a man's wealth was the breeding of the horses he owned. The arrival of summer visitors was often recorded in terms of their transportation. The quality of a man's team and carriage was a reliable indicator of his fortune.

In July of 1872, the *Long Branch News* observed,

> *William P. Ward of New York with his pair of trotters is at the Mansion House, Mr. T.F. Gilligan is now at the Ocean House with his dog cart. Mr. Rich has a pair of blacks and a laundolette with him at the West End. C.W. Chapin of New York has with him at the Pavilion a stylish phaeton, Daniel Drew of the Ocean House drives a fast pair of light horses, Mr. J.M. Atwater of Cooper Cottage drives a pair of South American pigmy ponies hitched to a miniature wagon. Mrs. O'Gilly of the Clarendon drives a large bay horse.*

William K. Vanderbilt was a regular gambler at Phil Daly's Pennsylvania Club on Brighton Avenue in West End. It was estimated that an average season saw between $5 and $10 million wagered in Daly's casino. James Connelly, a reporter for the *Long Branch News*, wanted to win the $100 prize that *Harper's Monthly Magazine* was offering for a three-hundred-word article on the richest man in the world. He asked Phil Daly to arrange an interview with Vanderbilt. The millionaire obliged and Connelly won the prize.

The patent medicine king Dr. H.T. Helmbold made his fortune selling Helmbold's Bachu Tea. He was one of the first businessmen to realize the potency advertising had for selling a product. He spent millions publicizing his tea as a secret brew from Africa, sure to cure whatever ails a person. He was a colorful character and wanted the world he lived in to be just as vibrant. He took a dislike to some of the older hotels that lined Ocean Avenue. He was rich enough to buy and tear them down so that his drive down the boulevard would be more enjoyable and well-suited to his high-stepping horses and flashy carriage. His home was on Chelsea Avenue. Due to bad investing and overspending he died penniless. His mental health declined and it is said that he spent his last days trying to sweep the sunshine off his front porch.

The wealthy Guggenheim family came to Long Branch in the late 1800s. They made their millions in the silver mines out west and spent most of it on the East Coast. When they were turned away from summering in Saratoga Springs because they were Jewish, they came to Long Branch, a town that had no religious boundaries. Long Branch was known by some as "The Jewish Newport, a resort on the stretch of the New Jersey Coast where distinguished bankers built overgrown cottages in simple, rustic style" as described in the book *Our Crowd*.

When the Guggenheims arrived from New York City they set a new tone to the town. Morris built a large Victorian-style mansion in West End. His three sons followed suit, with mansions of their own. Solomon Guggenheim built a renaissance palace named Firenze after his wife, Florence. Daniel built a Moorish-style fantasy home named El Diablo, and Murray copied the Petit Trianon in France for his home's style. The white marble mansion is now the Guggenheim Library on the campus of Monmouth University on the corner of Norwood and Cedar Avenues. Murray and Morris's homes were designed by the architectural firm of Carrere and Hastings. They were known worldwide for their works, one of the most famous being the New York Public Library on Fifth Avenue. Murray's niece, Peggy Guggenheim Seligman, who became the benefactor of the Guggenheim Museum in New York City, thought these homes overdone and did not like coming to Elberon. In particular, she did not like the landscaping and said, as recorded in *Our Crowd*, "The only flowers I remember were rambler roses, nasturtiums, and hydrangeas, and since then I have been unable to endure them."

Her grandfather, Joseph Seligman, was an old friend of both Presidents Grant and Garfield. His home was located right along the bluffs in Elberon. When Grant lost his investment in the Black Friday panic of 1869, his old card-playing buddy Seligman lent him money.

The Seligmans entertained often and elaborately. One of their guests, Prince Andre Poniatowsky, the nephew of King Stanislaus of Poland, was a weekend guest in Elberon. He said of his visit, "I entered a special world not quite like anything I had ever seen before in America or on the Continent." It was not an aristocracy that the Prince encountered in Elberon, but it was a gracious world that he would remember for a long time. Years later, he said that he had met people that weekend in Elberon, New Jersey, of whom no counterpart then existed in Europe, and probably no longer exists in America.

Samuel Sachs was related to the Guggenheim and Seligman families by marriage. He was the son-in-law of Marcus Goldman. The two men were partners in the Goldman Sachs investment firm. Sachs built a summer home in Long Branch and named it Ellencourt.

Bernard Baruch was a close friend of the Guggenheim family. His business sense helped save the family fortune by averting a mining workers' strike. The noted financier's family owned a thirty-five-room home in north Long Branch on Atlantic Avenue. It was known as the Anchorage. Baruch College in New York City is named for him. Judge Benjamin Cardozo, known as the Great Cardozo, owned a home on the oceanfront in Long Branch. The Cardozo School of Law in New York City is dedicated to him and his legal genius.

The Entertainers

With so much money and leisure time to spend, entertainment was the order of the day in Long Branch. Every famous name from the theater world came either to perform or to relax between engagements.

Maggie Mitchell was one of the premier actresses of her time. She gained fame in her role in *Fanchon, the Cricket*, a play written by George Sand. President Abraham Lincoln was one of her greatest fans. He watched her perform the part at Ford's Theatre on October 2, 1863. Henry James's first published work (in Boston's *Daily Traveller*) was a review of her acting skills. In 1875 she purchased a home on the corner of Norwood and Park Avenues in Long Branch and named it Cricket Lodge after the part she played for so long. Mitchell would continue acting in the role of the ingénue far into her old age.

Cricket Lodge was located in the Elberon section of town. Many of the actors visiting Long Branch stayed in the north end of town. Maggie Mitchell would often rent out her home in Elberon to actors seeking the sedate life and take up residence in the Murray Cottage, located on Atlantic and Branchport Avenues. Room and board was ten dollars a week. The cottage-hotel was an arrangement favored by theatrical people for a sort of no-strings-attached, bohemian existence. These boardinghouses were in a section of town known as Pleasure Bay on the Shrewsbury River. Gilbert and Sullivan operettas were often performed there on the famous floating stage.

Mitchell purchased her home from the actor James McVicker. He was the father-in-law of Edwin Booth. Booth was one of America's first great Shakespearean actors. He was the middle son of actors Junius and Agnes Booth. The family, which included the three brothers, were all in the theater. The younger and most handsome brother was John Wilkes Booth, who would gain fame not on the stage, but as the man who assassinated President Lincoln

The Booth Brothers were actors, most famous for their Shakespearean roles. Pictured from left to right: John Wilkes, Edwin and Junius Booth acting in a production of *Julius Caesar*. *Harvard Theatre Collection*.

Pleasure Bay Amusement Park was located on the banks of the Shrewsbury River in the north end of Long Branch. The circus-like sideshow was a favorite spot to watch balloon ascensions and take a turn at the shooting galleries and games of chance. *Author's collection.*

at Ford's Theatre. President Abraham Lincoln and his wife, Mary, had attended one of his performances there in 1863. In a strange twist, the entire Booth family, including John Wilkes, had acted together in 1864 at the Winter Garden in New York City. The play was *Julius Caesar.* Coincidentally, its theme was centered around a beloved leader being assassinated by one of his followers—a story neither of the other two brothers, Edwin or Junius Brutus Booth Jr., had any idea would become a reality in America. Edwin Booth built a home on Park Avenue in Long Branch, just west of Norwood Avenue where he was married in 1869. It was one of the first brick homes to be built in the city. His brother, Junius Jr., built his home on the oceanfront. His mother, Agnes, retired to this home.

Edwin Booth often performed on stage with Georgie Barrymore. She was the wife of Maurice and mother to the famous actors, Ethel, Lionel and John Barrymore. In the 1870s she was known as one of the best comedians of the day. She often stayed at the Riverside Hotel in Pleasure Bay and visited a nearby actors' colony in Little Silver. The entire Barrymore family made Long Branch their home for many summers.

Edwin Adams, hailed by his colleagues as one of the most outstanding thespians of his day, was the owner of a home in Long Branch named Sea View. It was located on the northwest corner of Park and Norwood Avenues.

The Wallacks—James W., Lester and Lester Jr. of the famous acting family—were among the most notable of Long Branch residents. Lester also owned the Wallack Theater on Broadway in New York. Their cottage was located in West End on Ocean Avenue. This was a typical summer day picturing the family relaxing outside. *Pat Curley Schneider.*

Many famous artists, poets and actors of the time were entertained there. Because of his popularity, Adams was invited to attend the grand ball that was given in President Grant's honor at the Stetson Hotel in the summer of 1869.

Lester Wallack and his cousin James are also part of Long Branch's theatrical past. They were both gifted actors living in Long Branch during the summer season. James bought the Lyceum Theater in New York City and renamed it the Wallack. He liked living in Long Branch and the commute to the city was a convenient one. He was referred to in a newspaper article as the "Pioneer settler among the dramatic people at the Branch. He came and others followed."

Frank Chanfrau made his fame and fortune on the Broadway stage. His wife, who acted under the name Mrs. Frank Chanfrau, sang in some of the original musical burlesque shows on Broadway. The Chanfraus' summer home, which they called the "Nest," was on Cedar Avenue in Long Branch. When asked by a *New York Sun* reporter what they did on vacation at the shore, Mrs. Chanfrau replied, "We all jump into our wagon every morning and go to our bath on the beach. Our bathing place is just below President Grant's. We see him and his family in the sea almost every morning. In the afternoon, we drive along Ocean Avenue or we stay at home and receive friends." Many of these friends were among the most famous actors of the day who were also summering in Long Branch.

The singer Lily Langtry was known as the Jersey Lily after the isle of Jersey in England where she came from. She was a regular visitor to Long Branch. When she came, she often used a Pullman Palace Car as her hotel. She would park it behind the railroad tracks on Bath Avenue and live in comfort all summer. Other times she stayed at the Catherine Hotel on Chelsea Avenue. Wherever she was residing, Langtry attracted attention. In 1883 she stunned the Long Branch locals when she took a dip in the ocean wearing a one-piece blue-and-red bathing suit. At this time, women were still expected to be covered from head to toe when they went swimming.

Fanny Davenport was the first burlesque queen, and she regularly brought her talents to Long Branch. She was an actress as well as an outspoken abolitionist. She counted among her friends and peers social reformers Henry Ward Beecher and Frederick Douglass, who were also summer visitors to the city.

Oliver Dowd Byron, president of Actor's Equity, owned a home on Ocean Avenue where he entertained local celebrities. He built fourteen cottages along the oceanfront as an investment and donated money to start a volunteer fire company named for him.

Lillian Russell, pin-up girl and actress, could often be seen being squired around town on the arm of her boyfriend, millionaire Diamond Jim Brady.

Nate Salsbury was a businessman turned showman. He knew a good investment when he saw one and Long Branch was it. He made lots of money and said he was "going to spend every cent of it in Long Branch." His home was on Liberty Street. At the turn of the century he built nine large homes on a tract of valuable land he owned on Troutman Avenue, now Joline Avenue. It was located near the ocean, and he named it the Reservation. Each home in the Reservation was named after a Native American tribe and the entrance drive was called the Trail. The Cherokee House is the only one of these historic homes left. It is the headquarters for a county-run beach known as Seven Presidents Park in North Long Branch.

The Florence Hotel, where Annie Oakley preferred the accommodations and had a famous shooting duel on the front lawn. *Durnell Collection.*

Another investment Salsbury made was in Buffalo Bill Cody's Wild West Show. The show was in debt and nearly out of money when Salsbury came along. He bought half an interest in the show. He eventually sold his share of the show to James A. Bailey, who later became a partner of P.T. Barnum, the circus promoter.

In addition to financial help, Salsbury assisted Buffalo Bill in matters of putting on a good show. In 1885 he hired sharpshooter Annie Oakley. For six years she was the star attraction in the show. Her specialty was shooting holes in playing cards tossed in the air. Chief Sitting Bull traveled with the show. He always called her "Little Sure Shot." Buffalo Bill Cody was a larger-than-life presence. He was a former Pony Express rider, buffalo hunter and Indian scout for General George Custer. He turned his horseback riding and roping skills into a traveling show of world renown.

Bill Cody and Annie Oakley both enjoyed coming to Long Branch. Oakley always stayed at the Florence Hotel on Ocean Avenue and North Broadway. In 1889 the owner of Phil Daly's casino in West End challenged her to a shooting match. It took place in front of the Florence Hotel and Annie Oakley won easily. Years later, when Phil Daly was in financial difficulty, Annie Oakley loaned him the money to pay the mortgages on seven homes he owned on Second Avenue, just north of his three-story mansion on the corner of Second and Chelsea Avenues. The site is now a parking lot for Star of the Sea Church.

Buffalo Bill and the members of his wild west show on their campgrounds on Morris Avenue. *Durnell Collection.*

Buffalo Bill and members of his Wild West Show stayed at Salsbury's Reservation in the summer and sometimes used it as a winter campground. The group also had campgrounds on Morris Avenue and on the corner of West End and Second Avenues. According to old route maps of the show's engagements, the show often came to Long Branch. They also used Long Branch as a home base when they were appearing in New York City or Philadelphia.

American Entertainer Dies in Long Branch

No history of the American circus is complete without the mention of Dan Rice. During most of the nineteenth century, Rice was a well-known entertainer, garnering the title of America's Most Famous Clown.

Even though Rice was born in New York City on January 25, 1823, his ancestry was connected to Monmouth County, New Jersey. When his will was probated in Freehold, New Jersey in 1900 it listed his address as 275 Norwood Avenue in Long Branch and his occupation as a comedian, a humorist—better known as a clown.

Dan Rice was more than a clown. He was a phenomenon, an inventor of himself and a new venue of show business that included singing, dancing, joke telling, equestrian stunts, animal taming and comical interactions with the audience.

Although funny for more than the half century his career spanned, Rice's life was not filled with quite as many lighthearted moments as his acts were. His start in life was shadowy and his final years were dim.

Born Daniel McLaren in New York City in 1823, his entrance into the world was not heralded. His mother's name was Elizabeth Crum. She was the daughter of an overbearing Methodist minister from Ocean, New Jersey. Seeking some adventure, she went to New York City in 1822. There she met a man named Daniel McLaren III at a horse race. He was a grocer who was less than upstanding in his business dealings and even less so when baby Daniel came along. There are no records of a McLaren-Crum marriage in New York or New Jersey, which suggests that Daniel was illegitimate.

Under these circumstances, Elizabeth and her son, whom she called Dandy Dan, returned to Long Branch where she had family. She soon married a local dairyman named Hugh Manahan. The marriage took place in 1825. For a short time life was good.

American Entertainer Dies in Long Branch

The family moved to New York and little Dan helped Manahan deliver milk in the Bowery and around the rowdy streets of New York City known as Five Points. There he started riding and training the horses that pulled the milk wagons. At this time, horse and man were matched together for transportation as well as a means to a livelihood. Little did Dan know that this relationship with animals was the start of a career that would introduce him to fame and fortune.

The brief stability in Dan's life soon ended when his mother died and Hugh Manahan remarried. He did not get along with his new stepmother, so he left home. He was only fourteen years old when he headed west, much like many young men of his time at the urging of Horace Greeley, the owner of the *New York Tribune*. Greeley's famous editorial spoke to them about a better life and the promise of gold in the west. Greeley was a summer resident of Long Branch, the home of his mother's family.

He worked his way west doing whatever came his way. For a time he was a stable boy where he used his horsemanship skills to work as a jockey. He also sang and danced for whatever audience he could find, collecting whatever they were willing to pay. He called himself Dusty Dan, and somewhere along the line he changed his name from Dan McLaren to Dan Rice. There are several theories for the name change. Some think he took the name of the man who owned the farm where he worked. Others are sure he had seen a famous British entertainer named Thomas Dartmouth Rice and simply borrowed the last name from him. However he got the name, it would someday become a draw for large audiences, important people and lots of money.

The first time Rice started to make real money was when he was traveling from town to town, performing with a "learned pig" named Lord Byron. When the pig answered questions from the audience or counted cards, it was done more by Rice's slight of hand than by the performing pig's intelligence.

While traveling with Lord Byron, Rice met Maggie Curran, a young girl from Pennsylvania. He was seventeen and she was eighteen when they got married. He and Maggie took to the road with their pet pig, picking up audiences, laughs and money wherever they could. They lived off the proceeds made by the learned pig. Of course, the pig was always fed first. Even then, Rice realized that being a showman involved more than tricks. It had its responsibilities as well.

When Lord Byron died, Rice had to revamp his act. He began singing and dancing while bantering with the audience. Many times he did it in black face, a common routine in the 1840s. He bounced around for five years doing whatever it took to get a laugh and pay the bills.

In 1845 Dan Rice got his big break. He began traveling with a real show for the first time, Nathan Howe's circus. It was also the first time he took on the role of clown. But he was not dressed in floppy shoes and a red nose. Dan fashioned his costume to look like the American Flag. It was made up of red-and-white striped leggings and a blue-and-white shirt. He also sported a stovepipe hat and grew a pointed goatee. It is said that Dan Rice was the inspiration when New Jersey resident and famous cartoonist Thomas Nast drew the caricature of Uncle Sam, the symbol of the United States and patriotism.

Rice's concept of humor was sophisticated. Much of his act had the intricacies of a Shakespearean play, with his performance entailing the high and mighty ringmaster ending up looking like a buffoon to Rice's sly upstaging. His act often involved horses. His equestrian ability, picked up from his days of delivering milk, was paying off.

In 1850 his wife, Maggie, gave birth in Long Branch to a daughter named Catherine. Maggie had come to the seaside town to stay with the Manahans, Rice's stepfather's family, while she was pregnant. Long Branch was still the place where Rice sought the comfort and security of home for him and his family. The only family he knew resided there. His sister, Libby, had married a local man named Jacob Showles. Jacob and Libby traveled with Rice from time to time. Libby did tricks with a hoop. The term hoopla was used to describe her act. Jacob rode the horses and performed stunts in the show.

For a time he made Girard, Pennsylvania, his home, but always gravitated back to the Jersey Shore. In 1857 Maggie and Dan divorced. When he remarried two more times, he brought each of his new brides back to Long Branch to meet his family and see the ocean.

After several years with Howe's circus, Rice began performing on riverboats, a popular venue of the time. He traveled up and down the rivers of the South. It is thought by many and seems most likely that one of these shows was seen in 1848 by a young Samuel Clemens, better known as Mark Twain. The then-twelve-year-old Clemens attended one of Rice's performances in Hannibal, Missouri. Years later, while writing *Huckleberry Finn*, Twain would include an entire chapter describing Huck's visit to a circus. This version is an exact recreation of the act Rice was performing at the time. Huck describes, "All the time, the clown carried on it most killed the people. The ringmaster couldn't ever say a word to him but he was back at him quick as a wink with the funniest things a body ever said; and how he ever could think of so many of them, and so sudden and so pat, was what I couldn't no way understand."

During his time on the Mississippi River with its millions of mosquitoes, Rice contracted yellow fever. It took him several months to recuperate, but he used this time to make plans and create some fables.

One of Rice's famous stories included the Whig candidate for president of the United States, Zachary Taylor. He had come to see one of Rice's shows while campaigning. Rice claimed that when he saw Taylor in the audience, he brought him down to the circus sawdust and put him on the bandwagon. He invited the rest of the audience to jump on the bandwagon and vote for Taylor for president. Rice lay claim to the political phrase "jumping on the bandwagon," which is still a popular expression today.

Rice was quick with his quips and always right on target. In 1857 the *Cincinnati Enquirer* complimented him: "His humors are adapted to the times, his hits local, his satire telling, his wit pointed…He is the great master-spirit of the nineteenth century the most amusing man of modern times."

By then he was the most renowned showman in the United States. His circus, called Dan Rice's Great Show, was crossing the country, playing to delighted crowds. His sister, Libby, and her husband, Jacob Showles, and stepbrother were permanent performers in the show along with his famous white horse, Excelsior. Animals were a big draw at the time. Excelsior performed the living statue as the opening act. The horse stood on a platform, which was carried on the shoulders of ten men, with his front hoof resting on a short platform. The horse never moved a muscle.

During the Civil War years, the population found respite in Rice's circus. Rice claimed that even Mary Todd Lincoln and President Lincoln attended one of his performances. He used politics in the ring not only as entertainment, but also as a way of letting people know how he felt about the war. He was against it morally, but supported the North. He gave money to families of soldiers off at war and outfitted an entire regiment of Erie, Pennsylvania soldiers. As many performers of the day did, he gave himself the title of colonel.

Through these years and the ones to follow many famous figures came into Rice's circus tent and in and out of his life. Fortunes rose and fell. It was said that Rice made $1,000 per week, twice as much as President Lincoln was making. When times were tough and he was in danger of losing his Pennsylvania property, his cousin W.C. Crum from Long Branch bought the acreage. This same cousin became treasurer for P.T. Barnum's Great Traveling Museum, Menagerie, Caravan and Hippodrome. It seems salt air and the smell of sawdust were in the genes of many of Rice's relatives.

Drinking, gambling and generosity took their toll financially on Rice and his great show. While setting up his tents in Camden, New Jersey, he couldn't afford to pay for the five dollars license needed to sell tickets. He was reduced to passing the hat at intermission. But when he came into some extra money, he presented the city of Newark, New Jersey, with a new fire truck.

At one time, when his cash was depleted, he was forced to perform with only one horse. Whenever he came into a new town, whatever the town's name, it would be called a "one horse town," which was another example of how Rice and his words seeped into American culture.

Whatever fate held for Rice, he always came back to the Jersey Shore for recharging. His sister, Libby, and her husband, Jacob Showles, had retired from the show and owned a livery stable and home in the West End section of Long Branch. Keeping the circus spirit alive, the Showles family kept their home open for the many circus performers that came through town. Long Branch was on the rise as a social and entertainment center, and many shows passed through town. Buffalo Bill Cody's Wild West Show visited the area often. Its location on the ocean was a big draw for these performers as well as Rice himself.

A newspaper photo shows Rice walking along the boardwalk overlooking the Atlantic Ocean. He was the image of gentility in a boater hat and carrying a cane—a scene Winslow Homer would have been eager to paint on one of his many visits to Long Branch during the late 1800s.

In 1875 Rice declared bankruptcy. Among his creditors were his daughter, Catherine, and her husband, A.C. Wurzbach, of Long Branch. His other daughter, Libby, was married to a painter from Long Branch named Charlie Reed.

For his finale, Rice returned to a small house on Norwood Avenue. Today, the Long Branch home, looks much as it did in 1880. The home belonged to Maria Brown, a spinster distantly related to Rice. Maria and her brother, John, took him in and she began helping write the memoirs of this once-famous clown.

Dan Rice died in Long Branch on February 22, 1900. The death certificate listed the cause of death as Bright's Disease, better known as nephritis, the inability of the kidneys to work properly. He was seventy-seven years old. His obituary appeared in the *New York Times* and the *Long Branch Record*. Today he is remembered by few, but at one time there was a Dan Rice day in Long Branch. Presidents sought out his comic relief, writers used his act as inspiration and performers copied his showmanship.

Dan Rice is buried in the Methodist cemetery on Locust Avenue in West Long Branch. A small white marker notes the spot, which rests in a corner of his family plot. His sister, Libby, and her husband, Jacob Showles, are buried nearby, although they have a larger headstone. His lasting monument is small and square, with the name Dan Rice nearly unrecognizable. But it is in no way indicative of the life he led as America's Most Famous Clown, which was neither small nor mundane.

Writers and Artists
Drawn to the Sea

With so many famous people in one place, Long Branch became a favorite destination for artists, writers and public commentators. Long Branch in its golden years supplied plenty of copy for newspaper reporters and writers, beautiful scenery for artists and a steady stream of interesting people to use as subjects. Many reformers and orators of the day were attracted to the city with its concentrated cluster of fame and fortune.

Noted artist Albert Bierstadt, who specialized in painting landscapes ensconced in fog and atmosphere, came to Long Branch for its seaside inspiration. Granville Perkins, who made many engravings for *Harper's Weekly*, was a regular observer of what was going on in the city. One of his engravings, entitled *Ocean Avenue*, appeared in *Harper's* in 1872 showing a typical scene along the well-traveled street.

Winslow Homer often came to Long Branch to capture scenes along the bluffs and on the beaches. One of his famous paintings, *On the Bluff in Long Branch at the Bathing Hour*, hangs in the Boston Museum of Fine Arts. It depicts handsomely dressed women looking down on the beach. In the background is a white flag, which was the signal that it was the bathing hour for proper young ladies. Another of his works entitled *On the Beach in Long Branch* depicts a woman carving the initials W.H. in the sand with an umbrella. He depicted himself as an unconcerned onlooker, but in reality he painted himself into the scene for a reason: he was watching a young teacher from Long Branch and she was writing his initials. The story is that they had a seven-year love affair which greatly influenced his work. During those years he devoted much of his artistic talent to capturing the ambiance of the seaside city.

So many artists came to Long Branch during the late 1800s that it was known as the American Boulogne, comparing it to the area in France where Manet went

Winslow Homer was a frequent visitor to Long Branch its beaches. This is one of his most famous wood engravings entitled *On the Beach, Long Branch. Author's collection.*

to self-invigorate and gain inspiration from the beautiful sea. Political observer Thomas Nast often used Long Branch and its famous residents as fodder for his satirical cartoons.

It was while President Grant was here in Long Branch that he began writing his own Civil War memoirs. Mark Twain paid him several visits and ultimately offered to publish the book so that it would earn a profit for the financially strapped, ailing president. The publication of the book helped support Mrs. Grant after her husband's death. It is known as one of the finest memoirs dealing with the aspect of war.

The poet Walt Whitman often visited Long Branch. On July 28, 1881, he wrote "My Native Sand and Salt Once More" about a trip he took, beginning,

> *8½ A.M., on the steamer Plymouth Rock, foot of 23d Street, New York for Long Branch. Another fine day, fine sights, the shores, the shipping and bay—everything comforting to the body and spirit of me. An hour later—Still on the steamer, now sniffing the salt very plainly-the long pulsating swash as our boat steams seaward—the hills of Navesink and many passing vessels—the air the best part of all. At Long Branch the bulk of the day, stopt at a good*

Horace Greeley, reformer and owner of the *New York Tribune*. *Durnell Collection*.

hotel, took all very leisurely, had an excellent dinner, and then drove for over two hours about the place, especially Ocean Avenue, the finest drive one can imagine, seven or eight miles right along the beach. In all directions costly villas, palaces, millionaires—(but few among them I opine like my friend George W. Childs, whose personal integrity, generosity, unaffected simplicity, go beyond all worldly wealth.)

Whitman writes about George Childs, also mentioned frequently by President Grant as a neighbor, friend and confidant.

Horace Greeley, the owner of the *New York Tribune*, was a regular summer visitor to the shore. Greeley helped establish the Republican Party and used his newspaper as a forum to advocate his positions on antislavery, labor unions and temperance. His was the first national newspaper to circulate by rail and steamboat lines, helping to unite the country in post–Civil War programs.

Henry Ward Beecher, the famous minister and antislavery speaker, often came to Long Branch as did others interested in what was happening in the South in the days following the Civil War. His sister, Harriet Beecher Stowe, was the famous writer of *Uncle Tom's Cabin*. President Lincoln said that her book was the impetus for the Civil War.

Mansions by the Sea

All of these well-known people, whose reputations remain larger than life, wanted to show off their wealth, their creativity and their social standing and found no better spot to do so than in Long Branch. It was the place to indulge in lavish living, lush housing and leisurely activities. They wanted all the show and splendor that money and power could buy.

The famous New York City architectural firm of McKim, Mead and White catered to much of the local clientele. Stanford White designed the Franklyn cottage where President Garfield died, as well as the Elberon Hotel. He also designed the second Madison Square Garden and the famous Washington Square Arch in New York.

The Continental Hotel in West End advertised itself as the largest hotel in the United States and contained six hundred rooms, an extra long bar, ballroom, billiard salon, bowling alleys and a shooting gallery.

Until the 1880s, hotels served as the focal point of resort life. Many social connections were made, kept and rekindled in them. President Grant was usually seen on the porch of the Elberon Hotel smoking and socializing. President Arthur liked to gamble in the hotels. His favorite was Phil Daly's Pennsylvania Club, located on Ocean and Brighton Avenues. The green cloth of the gambling tables attracted the Wall Street clientele who were used to wagering large sums on the stock market. Placing bets in Long Branch was a busman's holiday for them. Ladies and locals were not allowed to gamble in these establishments. When Phil Daly noticed a Long Branch resident inside his club, he gave him back the money he had lost and escorted him out.

Each hotel had its own brass band. They played on the lawn during the day and at mealtime. They played while the guests were eating so they would not hear the clang of pots and dinner plates coming from the kitchen.

Phil Daly's Pennsylvania Club was one of most famous casinos of its day. Located on Brighton and Ocean Avenues in West End, wealthy patrons flocked here and wagered large sums. Between $5 and $10 million passed hands each season. Local residents and women were not allowed to gamble in this establishment. *Author's collection.*

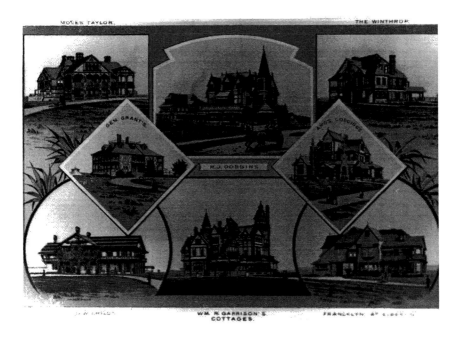

Mansions by the sea. *Author's collection.*

Monmouth Park from the Grandstand. *Harper's Weekly.*

In 1870 Monmouth Park opened. Built by John Chamberlain, a local gambling house owner, it was one of the premiere racetracks in the nation. Many of the most famous people of the day were there on opening day, July 4, 1870. An article in *Turf, Field, and Farm* described the grandstand as one of the most magnificent of its kind in the country, capable of seating several thousand people and situated that the horse racing could be seen without rising from one's seat. The first series of races at Monmouth Park ended with an event known as the Tweed Compliment. It was a consolation prize opened only to horses that were beaten. Its cash prize was offered by a track regular, Boss William Tweed, the corrupt New York City political power broker.

Shipwrecks Along the Sandy Shore

Traveling by steamship was the way most New York visitors chose to visit Long Branch. These vessels were so well appointed that the summer vacation began as soon as the boat left the dock.

The line of steamships owned by Jim Fisk were so elaborate that they were known as floating palaces. The *Plymouth Rock* was the fanciest of them all with fine dining, music and lounging areas onboard. Originally these boats would dock at Sandy Hook, and travelers would have to board stagecoaches or a local rail line for the final leg of their trip to Long Branch. Building a pier directly into the ocean in Long Branch seemed a way to make travel time quicker. The steamships could dock right there and passengers would be able to walk from the pier right to their hotels or waiting carriages.

Jim Fisk and Jay Gould were eager to build such a pier. However, it was wooden and not stable enough to hold up to a summer storm. It was washed away by a storm one week after its completion in 1872, and it was not until 1878 that another pier was built, this one opposite the Ocean Hotel (formerly the Continental Hotel). The Ocean Pier was six hundred feet long and was made of tubular iron, except at the ocean end where wood was used. It was ten pilings wide. Underneath were six hundred bathing cabins and the promenade deck above was covered with striped awnings and illuminated by large gas fixtures on tall ornamental posts. Benches and refreshment booths lined the pier. Regular excursion boats from New York used the pier as a landing place. It was a wonderful point of entry to Long Branch, until 1881, when it was destroyed by an angry Atlantic Ocean.

If this iron structure could not withstand a summer storm, how were seagoing vessels going to stay afloat? It was a question confronted every summer in Long Branch. Each boat and passenger was at the mercy of the weather and

Shipwrecks Along the Sandy Shore

The choppy waters along the Long Branch shore could prove perilous for boats. *Long Branch Historical Association.*

the stormy sea. Long Branch and her coastline were fickle hosts, sometimes welcoming and other times foreboding. If a visitor was caught in the middle of one of these mood swings while out at sea, it could prove to be a deadly situation.

New Jersey Governor William Newell recognized the need to help these stranded ships and introduced a bill encouraging the endowment of lifesaving stations to Congress in the early 1850s. When Mrs. Lincoln visited Long Branch in 1861, Newell was eager to show her how his techniques could save passengers and crew of shipwrecks from drowning. His bill was finally passed in 1871, and Congress created an official lifesaving service. He is known as the Father of the United States Lifesaving Service. Long Branch was a logical spot for a lifesaving station because so many ships were wrecked off its coast.

One of these shipwrecks occurred in 1859 when a strong southwest gale drove the Dutch ship *Adonis* aground in Long Branch. Waves pounded the wooden ship until she broke in half shortly after midnight. Sailors on the cargo ship were saved by volunteer rescue worker Charles Green and his crew. The *Monmouth Democrat* reported, "The daring and impulsive rescue boat's crew could not stand tamely by and see a carload of human beings in this doubtful situation, but rushed in up to their armpits, seized the car and brought it ashore. The lifesaving crew should be written in letters of gold upon the record of the Lifesaving Association."

The names of many famous ships and their wreckage are forever forged upon Long Branch's shores. They include the cargo ships *Dora Baker* and *Hannah*. The American liner *St. Paul* was loaded with $1.3 million in gold bullion and mail when she nosed her way through a blinding fog into the sand off Long Branch.

Cork vests were the lifejackets of the day. They were buoyant enough to keep the rescuers afloat in rough waters. *Author's collection.*

A surfboat was smaller and lighter than a lifeboat. It was mounted on a wheeled carriage and pulled through the sand to the site of the wreck. The surfboat could be launched from the beach and was able to cut through the breaking waves to rescue passengers, crew and sometimes cargo onboard the ships in distress. *Pat Curley Schneider.*

On March 7, 1859, the ship *Adonis* beached off the coast of Long Branch shortly before midnight carrying crew and cargo, but no passengers. Twenty years later, the steamer *Rusland* struck the remains of the *Adonis* and wrecked. *Rutgers University Special Collections and Archives.*

The Norwegian ship *Hannah* went aground near Long Branch on February 16, 1879. Lifesavers rescued all seventeen crew and sheltered thirteen of them at the lifesaving station for more than a month. *Author's collection.*

Lake Takanassee, Long Branch. N. J.

Three of the original lifesaving buildings can be seen just over the Takanassee Bridge in Elberon. This was the location of the first all-volunteer coastal lifesaving stations in the United States. Although no longer used in an official manner, these historic buildings still stand in the same spot watching over the sea. *Author's collection.*

She was racing the Cunard liner *Compania* into port in New York when she went off course. Many transatlantic liners raced each other to cut minutes off their times, so they could advertise the fastest Atlantic crossing. These races often ended in tragedy, and not the hoped-for victory.

The *New Era* is perhaps the most well known of these ships. On November 13, 1854, she was making her maiden voyage from Germany to New York when she found herself in the middle of a violent storm off the coast of Long Branch. With 427 passengers aboard, the ship was tossed and turned by stiff winds and strong surf. Despite the valiant efforts of the local lifesaving service, 284 lives were lost, some of them unidentified. They are buried in a mass grave in the United Methodist Cemetery in West Long Branch. A large monument was erected in the memory of those lost onboard one of the worst shipwrecks in this area's history.

The original all-volunteer lifesaving station in Long Branch consisted of three buildings. These historic buildings are still standing today. They are located on Ocean Avenue, on the property of the Takanassee Beach Club.

The Salt of the Earth

There are a group of Long Branch residents that are not remembered by name today, but they played a large role in making the town the popular resort it was. They are the domestics, groundskeepers, farmers, hotel workers and shop owners who worked behind the scenes to keep the town glittering in its golden days.

Many of these workers were German, Italian and Irish immigrants who were eager to work for an honest day's wage. They were not interested in promoting their popularity or making political connections and business deals. They took pride in their positions, which for many of them meant working in the homes of the most famous of Long Branch's residents.

One of these workers was Anna Elise Lenahan. She was a young girl from Limerick, Ireland. Arriving in Long Branch in the late 1860s from Ellis Island, she found a job in a summer cottage located at 991 Ocean Avenue. The home was owned by President Grant and his family. Since it was a cottage and did not require a large staff, Anna probably assumed more than one role in running the house, but her official title was that of a domestic.

A welcome respite from the social whirl of Washington, the Grants lived a simple, relaxed lifestyle while at Long Branch. They preferred eating the locally grown fruits and vegetables and especially enjoyed the seafood caught by the local fishermen. The ocean abounded in bluefish, mackerel and soft-shell crabs. Much of the town's economy revolved around the natural resources the ocean provided.

The Grant family brought along their Italian steward Melah, who supervised all of the White House entertaining. In Long Branch he planned the menus, but most likely it was one of the local cooks who actually prepared the meals.

President Grant ate fried apples every day and also enjoyed rice pudding. He did not like poultry or rare meat. His favorite summer breakfast included broiled

Anna Lenahan Brown. *Author's collection.*

Spanish mackerel, whole wheat bread, steak, bacon, fried apples, buckwheat cakes and strong coffee. Anna Lenahan most likely prepared some of these meals because she was used to preparing simple food, using what grew in the farms and gardens and came from the dairies in town.

In those days there were no vacuum cleaners, so Anna used an old Irish method of cleaning the floors: she would pour tea leaves on the carpets and

This scene depicts a fishing boat coming into shore with its catch of the day. The catching, selling and eating of fish were daily occurrences in Long Branch. Because of its proximity to the ocean and the choice of fish, which included mackerel, blue fish and flounder, this was a way for many locals to make a living. *Author's collection.*

Everyone loved the beach in Long Branch. *Pat Curley Schneider.*

sweep them off along with the dust, crumbs and probably a good deal of sand brought in after a day on the beach.

During the winter when the Grants returned to Washington, she found work in the local hotels and boardinghouses. While working at the Grant cottage she met one of the groundsmen named Frank Brown. He was from the area of Long Branch known as the "big woods." It is now known as Ocean Township. In those

Lewis B. Brown, the developer of Elberon, had a home on the corner of Sycamore and Ocean Avenues. *Durnell Collection.*

Ocean Boulevard. *Author's collection.*

days anything west of Norwood Avenue was accorded this term because it was mostly undeveloped, forested land.

They got married and Frank found a job at a local establishment, Eiseles's Florists. They built a small house at 264 West End Avenue and took in boarders to earn extra money.

For milk and eggs, Anna kept a cow and two chickens named Mollie and Moochy on her small piece of property and continued to make fried apples, fried potatoes and many loaves of whole wheat bread every day. And her tea leaves never went to waste. She continued to use them to sweep the floor and sometimes tell fortunes with the ones that collected at the bottom of the tea cup.

Although she did not dedicate an expensive altar, statue or stained glass window to St. Michael's Roman Catholic Church, she was one of the first local residents to donate money to build it. When Anna and a group of friends began worshiping there, the church was a simple wood structure with a dirt floor.

Today, the name Anna Elise Lenahan Brown is remembered only by her family, who still live in Long Branch five generations later. But it was people like her and the force of local laborers who made it possible for presidents to summer here, millionaires to build and maintain mansions, hotels to serve up to four hundred dinners in one night and host a grand ball for a First Lady, groom and stable the legion of horses that arrived every summer and help keep the town of Long Branch shining during its golden years.

Selected Bibliography

Ackerman, Kenneth. *Dark House: The Surprise Election and Political Murder of President James A. Garfield*. New York: Carroll and Graf, 2003.

Baker, Jean H. *Mary Todd Lincoln: A Biography*. New York: Norton and Company, 1987.

Birmingham, Stephen. *Our Crowd*. New York: Harper and Row, 1967.

Buchholz, Margaret. *Shore Chronicles*. Harvey Cedars, NJ: Down the Shore Publishing, 1999.

Carlyon, David. *Dan Rice: The Most Famous Man You've Never Heard Of*. Cambridge, MA: Perseus Books Group, 2001.

Carr, William. *The duPonts of Delaware: A Fantastic Voyage*. New York: Dodd, Mead and Company, 1964.

DuPont letters, Eleutherian Mills Historical Library, Greenville, Delaware.

Frank Leslie's Illustrated Magazine.

Harper's Weekly.

Leech, Margaret. *The Garfield Orbit*. New York: Harper and Row, 1978.

Long Branch News.

McFeely, William. *Grant: A Biography*. New York: Norton, 1974.

Monmouth County Historical Association Library and Archives.

Monmouth Inquirer.

Moss, George H. *Steamboat to the Shore*. Sea Bright, NJ: Ploughshare Press, 1966.

———. *Victorian Summers at the Grand Hotels of Long Branch, New Jersey*. Sea Bright, NJ: Ploughshare Press, 2000.

New Jersey Writers Project. *Entertaining A Nation: The Career of Long Branch*. New Jersey: Works Project Administration, 1940.

New York Herald.

New York Times.

Philadelphia Public Ledger.

Roberts, Russell. *Down The Jersey Shore*. New Brunswick: Rutgers University Press, 1953.

Taylor, John M. *Garfield of Ohio: The Available Man*. New York: Norton, 1970.

Turner, Justin G., and Linda Levitt Turner. *Mary Todd Lincoln, Her Life and Letters*. New York: Fromm International, 1987.